# ASSESSING ADOPTIVE AND FOSTER PARENTS

# ASSESSING ADOPTIVE AND FOSTER PARENTS

Improving Analysis and
Understanding of Parenting Capacity

Edited by
Joanne Alper and David Howe

Foreword by John Simmonds

Jessica Kingsley *Publishers*
London and Philadelphia

First published in 2015
by Jessica Kingsley Publishers
73 Collier Street
London N1 9BE, UK
and
400 Market Street, Suite 400
Philadelphia, PA 19106, USA

*www.jkp.com*

**Library of Congress Cataloging in Publication Data**
Assessing adoptive and foster parents : improving analysis and understanding / edited
by Joanne Alper
and David Howe.
    pages cm
  Includes bibliographical references and index.
  ISBN 978-1-84905-506-2 (alk. paper)
  1. Adoptive parents. 2. Adopted children. 3. Foster home care. 4. Foster parents. 5.
Foster children.
  6. Social work with children--United States. I. Alper, Joanne. II. Howe, David, 1946-
  HV875.A76 2015
  362.73'3--dc23
                          2014039689


**British Library Cataloguing in Publication Data**
A CIP catalogue record for this book is available from the British Library

ISBN 978 1 84905 506 2
eISBN 978 0 85700 915 9

*For Ian, Evie and Lily*

# CONTENTS

# FOREWORD

*John Simmonds*

Creating a family life for a child through adoption or fostering is in many respects quite extraordinary. It is probably a heartfelt conviction for most of us that 'falling in love' with a baby naturally brought into the world is fundamental to their development and wellbeing. We have come to understand in a lot of detail what 'falling in love' might mean, why it is so important and what some of the complexities might be but the detail of the science cannot obscure the power of that fundamental belief in the place of love. Family placement, especially permanent family placement – whatever the legal order that might frame it – relies quite heavily on the power of love even if it might be more comfortably expressed using concepts like 'attachment'. Becoming a carer or facilitating somebody to become a carer has at its heart the intimate, intricate world of human relating and relationships. It is this that children expect and need and it is our responsibility to provide it.

We know, and this is conveyed very powerfully in the chapters in this book, that 'falling in love' may not be so straightforward when children have been removed from their birth parents and placed in foster care or for adoption. It is likely that those children will have adapted to a series of significant adversities in their lives – both pre and post birth. Their expectations of the world and particularly the people in their lives will have defensively adjusted to these adversities. The degree to which it is possible and what it takes for children to re-adjust to more hopeful and positive expectations are difficult questions for professionals, adopters and foster carers. We know from experience that many children do positively adjust but for some this only happens to a very limited extent and the impact on carers in terms of their subsequent re-adjustment – stress, disappointment, conflict or maybe breakdown – can be very demanding.

The focus of this book is on one critical aspect of these challenging questions: the assessment of prospective adopters and foster carers. There could not be any more significant professional task than to assess and then make a prediction of what is likely to happen if prospective carers are approved and then have a child or children placed with them. As this book makes clear, it is part art and to a limited extent, science. We have come to understand something of the challenge for these carers and indeed for the children but we are relying on our sense of what the issues are and what they are likely to become rather than any sense of being able to predict outcomes with certainty. The one thing that is absolutely clear is that the process of assessment and approval is only the beginning of a life journey – it opens the door and for some it may close it, but what is to be found on the other side needs as much, if not more, attention, time, resources and support.

Each one of these chapters discusses in considerable detail what the current state of play is both for the art and the science of assessment. We need more people to 'fall in love' with these vulnerable children and answering the question of what the role of the professional is to be in their task of enabling this could not be more important.

*John Simmonds*
Director of Policy, Research and Development,
British Association for Adoption and Fostering

# ACKNOWLEDGEMENTS

This book would not have been possible without the generous help and support of a number of people. I should therefore like to thank the following. First and foremost, I would like to thank Deborah Ferguson and Paul Snell, founders of Adoptionplus, without whom none of this would have been possible. I should also like to thank all my colleagues at Adoptionplus, with particular thanks to Stuart Campbell, Steve Haddrell, Claire Grady, Pippa Bolger, Ben Gurney-Smith and Elsie Price. It continues to be a pleasure to work with so many engaged and committed people. Dr John Simmonds, Director of Policy, Research and Development at British Association for Adoption and Fostering (BAAF), has been a willing source of both information and encouragement. Dr Kim S. Golding, too, has been unstinting in her thoughts and suggestions about how the book might be improved and developed. Thank you, John and Kim. I also would like to express my gratitude to Michelle Sleed, Senior Research Tutor at the Anna Freud Centre, for the help she has given me to think more clearly about the concept and practice of reflective functioning. Additionally, although they might not have been aware of their contribution, I should like to thank all the social workers I have met over the years on the training courses that I have run. Their ideas, responses and experiences have helped shaped my thinking and understanding regarding the assessment process. My thanks would not be complete without also acknowledging the influence of the families we have worked with and how much I have learnt from them. And finally, a big thanks to my husband, Ian and my two daughters, Evie and Lily. Writing and editing this book has inevitably eaten into home life, so I have needed their love and support to see this project through.

*J.A.*

# CHAPTER 1

# Introduction

*Joanne Alper*

This book has been designed to be helpful to busy social workers who are committed to working effectively, perceptively and supportively with prospective adopters and foster carers. Assessing prospective adoptive and foster parents poses many challenges for practitioners keen to find and support parents for children. In our assessments, we have to understand the needs of adopted children, be clear about the qualities needed in parents and ensure that people feel comfortable talking about these matters. We have to be able to write about all of this clearly and concisely in a report submitted to a panel. And all of this has to be completed within a specified time limit. Additionally, we have the complexities and vagaries of human nature with which to contend as we recognise that different people behave differently under the stresses and strains of parenting. Parenting an adopted or foster child, of course, can bring its own particular demands and challenges. How is a particular adult, whether they have had experiences of being a parent or not, likely to respond to these special, usually unanticipated challenges? How can we, as social workers, assess their likely responses and help them as adoptive parents understand and imagine themselves in these as-yet-unknown parenting situations?

As a social worker working in this field for a number of years I thought that it would be helpful to bring together a small group of key international experts who could help shed light on some of the dilemmas we face and deepen our understanding of the process of analysis and assessment. Given current thinking in developmental theory and research, it seems clear that understanding the links between our brains, our responses, our own attachment patterns and our relationship experiences can enhance the way we think about, understand and assess people as prospective adopters. In order to ensure that we do the best job possible, I want to argue that the assessment process is not just about whether someone should be approved as an adoptive or foster parent, but also about what strengths and vulnerabilities they are likely to bring to their parenting role. Specifically, we need to recognise and understand how they would be likely to react and cope under stress, and anticipate what skills and supports they would find most helpful at such times.

The skills required of the social worker in carrying out this work are of a high order. As professionals, we are responsible for providing parents for children who have already suffered significant hurt by their birth parents. Parents who should have been there to love them, care for them and protect them have neglected them and harmed them. It's difficult to imagine how children in these traumatic situations begin to make sense of and resolve these deeply damaging experiences.

Fostering and adoption offer these children a second chance: a second chance to understand and experience what it is like to be truly cared for and safely looked after, what it is like to be meaningfully and lovingly connected to another human being, what it is like to be able to rely on them and experience a healthy relationship, and what it is like to be able to regulate and manage your feelings in the context of a caring relationship. Adoptive and foster families have the chance to make a huge, immeasurable impact on the whole life of another human being. As social workers, we can play a central role in making those chances happen.

It's worth considering the history of adoption and fostering and how this has shaped how we work today. Forms of adoption and fostering have always existed in the United Kingdom in the sense of people taking other people's children into their homes and looking after them on a permanent or temporary basis. Fostering, where a child lives temporarily with another family, began to be regulated from the middle of the 19th century onwards, following a series of 'baby farming' scandals. However, adoption, the permanent removal of a child into another family, had no legal basis in the United Kingdom until the 20th century. In 1926 the first legislation relating to adoption was passed, and since then almost every decade has seen new laws introduced that increasingly regulate the process. Initially children came in to the system as the result of social stigma associated with poverty or being an unmarried mother. The peak number of adoptions was in 1968, since when there has been an enormous decline. From the 1960s, social, cultural, economic and legal changes have meant that the majority of children who are now adopted in the United Kingdom are mainly from local authority care, where they have been looked after as a result of abuse and neglect experienced within their birth families.

From around the 1970s it was thought that the provision of a loving home would be sufficient to help 'deprived' and 'damaged' children to heal. At this time the preparation element of the assessment process was highlighted. There was an understanding that new ways needed to be found to explore this. Inherent in the concept of preparation was the idea that applicants could change and grow during the process of assessment and placement, and that agencies had a responsibility to help them develop. Alongside this, assessing a couple for adoption or fostering was seen as something that took place via the relationship between the couple and the social worker. Considerable time was made available for the social worker to build a trusting relationship and get to know the family. This relationship and the trust the couple had in the social worker were also seen as invaluable throughout the matching and post-placement support process.

There was another change of focus in the 1980s following a number of high-profile child protection enquiries. These highly publicised enquiries encouraged the social work profession to develop a more defensive style of practice. I believe that this, together with the introduction of the Community Care Act in 1989 and the Purchaser/Provider split (a change within the internal structure of local authorities where the assessment of what services were needed and the provision of those services were separated out), promoted a significant change in social work practice. It could be argued that there was a move away from a relationship-based approach to social work practice in which practitioners worked alongside people and understanding situations from their perspective.

Skills in psychological and emotional understanding were replaced by more structured 'box ticking' assessment forms as social workers sought to 'cover their backs' and avoid the public pillorying that some of their colleagues had experienced when things had gone wrong. Around this time, local authorities also made organisational changes, splitting child care teams into 'specialisms'. This appears to have further moved the social work professional away from a relationship-based, holistic approach to a way of working that was focused on a particular problem or moment in time. All of this seems to have influenced adoption and fostering assessments, encouraging a move away from relationship-based assessments to ones of guidelines and checklists. It could also be argued that the devaluing of the social work profession, both in the media and in the courts, additionally encouraged social workers to devalue their own interpersonal analytical skills, and instead resort to a format of process recording when undertaking assessments.

This has led to criticism in recent years that prospective adoptive and foster parent reports focus too much on process recording and not enough on analysis. The British Agency of Adoption and Fostering (BAAF) recognised the need for social workers to focus more on analysis when undertaking assessments, and have added analysis sections to their Parent Assessment Report (PAR) to encourage it. In 2010 BAAF published *Making Good Assessments: A Practical Resource Guide* by Pat Beesley (2010). Beesley writes, 'A common criticism of social work assessments has been that they lack good analysis.' She goes on to say 'an analytical approach to assessment should be evident from the start of the assessment' and that 'reflective practice is key'. BAAF also recognises the importance of the relationship between the social worker and parent, and the skills of the social worker.

The reality is that adoption and fostering are all about people and relationships. In order to assess if an individual has the capacity to adopt or foster, you have to really understand them. The best and most effective way to do this is in the context of the relationship between the social worker and the prospective adoptive or foster parent. If we accept that the relationship between the social worker and parent is central to the quality of the assessment, we also need to recognise that the social worker also brings all of his or her humanity into the room with them. Increasingly, social workers in the UK have less and less time to get to know people. It is clearly more difficult to build a trusting relationship in a shorter space of time. However it is something that we must try to do if we are to know people and understand how they will parent. The skills of the social worker become even more critical in the assessment situation. Social workers need strong interpersonal skills as well as key knowledge and understanding if they are going to be able to undertake assessments that are analytical and supportive in character.

If we want to ensure that we use the limited time we have as effectively as possible, it is essential we understand what qualities are important in parenting children who have experienced abuse and neglect, and the part we can play as social workers in recognising and promoting these qualities.

Central to these assessments and to this book is to understand the parenting needs of children who have suffered developmental trauma. Children who have been neglected and hurt by their birth parents not only require a different style of parenting, but also require parents to possess certain key qualities. Understanding the needs of children who have experienced abuse and neglect should underpin all of our parenting assessments. We need to not only keep the child in mind throughout the assessment process, but also keep their unique needs in mind as well. In Chapter 2, Kim S. Golding identifies and explores these unique needs and explains the underlying reasons for them.

In Chapter 3, Julie Selwyn looks at research from a number of countries which has examined and assessed the importance that assessments play in identifying suitable adoptive and foster parents. Joanne Alper, in Chapter 4, explores the development of the assessment process in the design and set up of Adoptionplus, a new voluntary adoption agency. This is followed by Kim S. Golding and Ben Gurney-Smith who, in Chapter 5, consider the qualities needed to successfully parent children who have experienced developmental trauma. In Chapter 6, Dan Hughes examines the importance of prospective adopters' and foster carers' own attachment patterns in understanding not only how they will parent, but also importantly, how they will parent when feeling under stress. In Chapters 7 and 8 Jonathan Baylin looks at how the brain and the vagal system react both under stress and in the context of caring relationships, followed by a discussion of the importance of reflective functioning in parent–child relationships and how it can be assessed. Finally, in a Conclusion, David Howe identifies some of the book's key themes and messages, before drawing the threads together.

## Reference

Beesley, P. (2010) *Making Good Assessments: A Practical Resource Guide*. London: BAAF Publications.

# CHAPTER 2

# Why Are You Frightened of Being Parented?

## Understanding Developmental Trauma

*Kim S. Golding*

Six-year-old Jenny lives in a loving home with her parents and younger sister, Olivia. They are playing at the park one day when a dog gets away from his owner and runs into the playground. Excited by the novelty, the children start to chase him. The dog becomes more and more afraid, as he is cornered by the noisy children. Before either the dog's owner or Jenny's mother can reach the children, Jenny approaches the dog. Thoroughly unnerved and with nowhere to go, the dog growls and then bites Jenny on the arm. By the time their mum does get to them, both Jenny and Olivia are crying. Jenny subsequently needs three stitches in her arm.

This has been a scary experience for both girls and months later they are showing signs of a post-traumatic reaction. The girls have woken up upset following dreams that seem to involve dogs. They are vigilant when out, looking to see if there is a dog in the vicinity, and they become distressed if a dog approaches them. However, Mum and Dad are patient. They tell the story of the day Jenny's arm was bitten by a dog many times to the two girls. They also notice that the girls act out the scenario with their toys. They use this as an opportunity to show them how the parents and the doctors were on hand to help them, and that this kept them safe. Slowly and gradually they introduce the girls to a range of trusted dogs owned by friends. By the time Jenny is eight years old this incident is well behind them and the girls frequently pester for a dog of their own!

Jenny and Olivia experienced what is known as a single-event trauma. Jenny experienced an event that led to an injury and Olivia witnessed it. Both girls responded with some degree of fear, helplessness and horror. The event was extremely upsetting and in the short term overwhelmed the girls' internal resources (see Briere and Scott 2006). The girls had a post-traumatic reaction which included bad dreams, a preoccupation with the event, and a behavioural and biological response to reminders of the event such as when they saw another dog loose nearby (see van der Kolk 2005). Both girls recovered from this traumatic event, helped by the sensitive support of their parents. Whilst the story of the dog that bit Jenny became a family story that they repeated many times over the year, the girls were able to recover and enjoy being with dogs.

Compare Jenny and Olivia's experience to that of Andrzej. As a young child Andrzej witnessed the large-scale destruction of the city of Sarajevo during the Bosnian war for independence. He was exposed on a daily basis to the bombardment of the civilians by the Serb forces. He became used to staying alert for snipers on his daily trip out to collect bread and water for his family. He witnessed the death of his uncle and cousin when a bomb landed on the concrete block where their apartment was. Throughout this Andrzej experienced a sense of belonging within his community and being in the loving arms of his parents. His immediate family survived the siege but the experience left him troubled by his dreams even years later. Additionally, he has never lost the vigilance to danger that he developed during those war years. Even a distant car back-firing would have him running for cover. Despite this, Andrzej grew up to be a successful worker and parent. He was heavily involved in the rebuilding of the city.

Like Jenny and Olivia, Andrzej had a post-traumatic response to the experience of trauma in his childhood, but in his case this was complex trauma that exposed him to multiple traumatic events. This impacted upon him both at the time and in the longer term, affecting his health and his biological responses to reminders of his war-time experiences. However, with the support of family and community, he recovered well enough to lead a full and productive adulthood.

A key factor in Jenny and Olivia's recovery from a single-event trauma and Andrzej's recovery from complex trauma was the support of their parents. Sensitive, attuned parenting and a sense of being unconditionally loved provided a healthy relationship environment within which they could recover from the trauma experienced in childhood. The children were able to develop resilience because of the parenting that they experienced.

Children removed from their birth family rarely have this early parenting experience. Let us reflect on Matthew's life. Even before he was born he was hearing the violent arguments between his two parents. His mother could barely soothe herself; alert as she was for the next beating, she had no space to keep her developing baby in mind. Her high stress levels led to increased levels of the stress hormone, cortisol. This hormone crosses the placenta and bathes the developing foetus in a high cortisol environment, an indicator that the foetus needs to be readied for a stressful environment. Following his birth the arguments continued. Often Matthew was held between his warring parents. At least once he was wrenched from his mother's arms and flung onto the bed by his father. Matthew, as an infant, had an innate instinct to signal his distress to his parents, but when he did he was met at best with no response from his parents. Worse they yelled at him, told him to shut up and even on occasion hit him. Matthew learned not to signal when he needed soothing, but with no capacity to soothe himself all he could do was sleep through his distress. Matthew was moved in an emergency, in the middle of the night, to a foster placement. He was found to be a 'good' baby, no trouble to care for, spending a large amount of time asleep. When he 'woke up' in his toddler years he was highly active, prone to tempers and unusually self-reliant. He rarely turned to a parent for comfort, even when he experienced pain or distressing experiences.

Like Jenny, Olivia and Andrzej, Matthew has experienced trauma in his childhood. Similar to Andrzej, this is a complex trauma; the trauma has been chronic and prolonged, beginning early in life. However, unlike Andrzej, Matthew did not have parents he could trust to love and care for him. He had no support that he could rely on during the worst of his experience. Matthew had to learn to become self-reliant, an ability he clung to throughout his childhood. The complex trauma that Matthew experienced occurred within his family and this has had a major impact on him. This complex trauma has come to be called developmental trauma in recognition of the devastating impact it has upon a child's development (Cook *et al.* 2005; van der Kolk 2005).

Developmental trauma is sometimes called complex post-traumatic stress disorder (PTSD), but this diagnostic label is misleading because children can experience developmental trauma and not fulfil the criteria for a diagnosis of PTSD. Developmental trauma is a description that captures the devastating experience of multiple exposures to trauma from within the family over critical developmental periods resulting in multiple developmental difficulties (van der Kolk 2005).

Jenny, Olivia, Andrzej and Matthew have all experienced varying levels of trauma within their childhoods. They have all needed sensitive parenting, which could help them to recover from these traumatic experiences. This has been sufficient to allow Jenny and Olivia to fully recover. Andrzej has been able to recover to the extent that he has become a successful adult and a good parent, but the impact of the trauma he experienced will never fully leave him. Matthew has not recovered. The lack of sensitive parenting early in life has left him unable to benefit from sensitive adoptive parenting. His parents will need to provide therapeutic parenting over an extended period if he is to meet the successes in adulthood that Andrzej has achieved. Matthew's parents will need a degree of resilience, too, if they are to withstand the challenges that Matthew presents, and the impact that parenting a developmentally traumatized child can have.

The experience of developmental trauma is unfortunately common amongst the group of children who are freed for adoption or placed in foster care. An understanding of developmental trauma is therefore very important both for the prospective carers or parents who are making a decision to foster or adopt children and for the social workers who are involved in assessing the suitability of applicants. Social workers need to ensure that the prospective parents are given this information prior to starting an assessment. They will then better understand the assessment process and why certain qualities and capacities are being looked for within this assessment.

Social workers and prospective parents therefore need to be clear about the impact of trauma on children and on the adults that subsequently care for them. A good understanding of the experience of the children, the impact of this experience on development and the parenting challenges that this can present create an important context for assessing the capacity and resilience of the potential parents.

Potential parents will not only need to be able to understand the experience of the child and the impact of this on their behaviour, but also need to be prepared to adjust their parenting to take into account the impact of this early experience. Flexibility and adaptability in the face of challenges will be important attributes when parenting children who have experienced developmental trauma.

## The impact of developmental trauma on children and young people

Children are more likely to be exposed to intrafamilial trauma than to non-interpersonal traumas such as the one experienced by Jenny and Olivia (van der Kolk 2005). As we began to explore when considering the experience of Matthew, we recognized that being exposed to developmental trauma at such a young age has a devastating impact upon the subsequent development of the child. These children are highly vulnerable. They have an increased risk of lifelong problems that affect their behaviour, mental health, emotional well-being and their relationships.

This is especially so because of the immaturity of the brain at birth and its susceptibility to being influenced by the social environment in which it finds itself.

> The organizing, sensitive brain of an infant or young child is more malleable to experience than a mature brain. While experiences may alter the behaviour of an adult, experience literally provides the organizing framework for an infant and child. Because the brain is most plastic (receptive to

environmental input) in early childhood, the child is most
vulnerable to variance of experience during this time. (Perry
2002 p.88)

To understand the impact of developmental trauma, therefore, we
need to understand its influence upon the developing brain and in
turn upon the development of attachment relationships. This early
experience will impact upon the later experiences of the child.

Matthew, for example, had a brain that was wired for danger and
a lack of trust in others. He learnt how to behave with his birth
parents and this impacted upon his behaviour with his foster and later
his adoptive families. He was more self-reliant and less able to seek
comfort when distressed. He did not know how to use his parents
as a secure base from which he could successfully build relationships
outside of the home. This lack of security later meant he struggled
to cope with the learning and relationship demands of school. His
early experience was the foundation for ongoing difficulties with
his capacity for regulation. He found it difficult to calm down once
aroused. He struggled to self-reflect and make sense of his experiences
and relationships with others. He found it hard to trust others.

Briere (2002) describes child abuse and neglect as interrupting
normal child development. Normal negative emotional reactions
such as sadness, anger or worry become conditioned to triggers
reminiscent of the original experience. Matthew will experience
these emotional states more intensely when he perceives his parents
as being unavailable or, worse, if they argue or become stressed –
normal reactions to daily life, but for Matthew a reminder of the
more intense arguments and stress of his birth parents. In addition,
these conditioned reactions become generalized over time. Thus, even
a neutral expression on a parent's face or a parent telling him 'no' or
being displeased with him can cause these reactions, which can come
to signal fear resulting in a trauma response. This reinforces Matthew's
need to be self-reliant and moves him even further away from being
able to seek comfort from his parents when he experiences distress;
after all, from his perception it is his parents who are the source of
this distress and unavailable as comforters. Matthew's learnt responses

to his parents no longer allow them to attune to his emotional experience or to provide sensitive, responsive and nurturing care. Without this his development is affected. Without parental support Matthew is at risk of becoming too easily overwhelmed by emotional distress and, as a consequence, he develops a range of cognitive and emotional avoidance strategies. Ironically, these adaptive responses to a world that is perceived as threatening also interfere with the normal processes of healing from trauma.

Unlike Jenny, Olivia and Andrzej, Matthew is not able to use the support of his parents to recover from the original traumatic experience and desensitize his over-reactive nervous system.

It is no surprise that children exposed to trauma have almost double the rate of psychiatric disorders compared to those not exposed to trauma. This includes anxiety and depressive disorders, functional impairments, disruptions of important relationships and school problems (Fairbank 2008). The children most at risk are the children exposed to developmental trauma, children who are so challenged that they cannot allow their parents to assist in their recovery.

A group of researchers interested in the study of developmental trauma have summarized the core difficulties that can result from this early experience (Cook *et al.* 2005; van der Kolk 2005). These are summarized in Box 2.1. Children will need parenting support to help them recover in all the areas described if they are to heal from the trauma and fulfil their potential.

As we can see, developmental trauma can have a devastating impact on children in all areas of development. The cruel irony is that the children who need most help from their caregivers in order to recover from the trauma have a range of difficulties that negatively impact on their ability to elicit or use parental support. The children are difficult to parent and resistant to the support or help that parents can offer.

This is why it is so important that prospective parents are supported and helped to understand not only the complex range of difficulties that children bring with them, but also the potential impact these can have on them as parents.

## BOX 2.1 CORE DIFFICULTIES OF THE DEVELOPMENTALLY TRAUMATIZED CHILD

*Biological*: The trauma impacts on brain development, including the integration of left and right hemisphere brain functioning. This means that emotion overwhelms more easily as the calming power of rational thought is not accessible. The child is more susceptible to the effects of stress and can have ongoing difficulties in focusing attention and modulating arousal levels.

*Attachment*: The child develops insecure and/or disorganized attachment behaviours, which impacts on the capacity to elicit care when needed. This can result in either excessive dependency or excessive self-reliance, or a combination of the two.

*Affect regulation*: Children are easily overwhelmed by intense or numbed emotions. They are poor at emotionally regulating or at letting others help them with this.

*Dissociation*: In the absence of good emotional regulation the children develop dissociative strategies to cope. They learn to cut off from emotional experience, leaving it unregulated and non-integrated.

*Behavioural regulation*: As the children struggle to manage their emotional experiences this will have an impact upon how they manage their behaviour. This can lead to under-controlled behaviours demonstrated through an increase in aggressive and oppositional difficulties, or over-controlled behaviours displayed through overly compliant behaviours but also difficulties managing change in routines.

*Cognition*: Early difficulties also impact on cognitive development. This can lead to language difficulties, deficits in IQ, less flexible and creative problem solving and deficits in attention, abstract reasoning and problem solving.

*Self-concept*: Difficulties with emotional regulation, behaviour and cognition all take their toll on the child's developing sense of self. The children can lack a coherent sense of self and can experience themselves as ineffective, helpless, deficient and unlovable. They are also more likely to blame themselves for negative experiences and have difficulties eliciting or responding to the support of others.

Parents will need the capacity to understand complex, challenging and often quite perplexing behaviours in their children. They will need to be open to support from skilled practitioners who can join with them in making sense of the children. They will additionally need the emotional resources to retain this understanding under stress, and the self-awareness to know when emotional resources are running dry so that they can look after themselves and maintain some emotional resilience.

Parents who are open to self-care and recognize the importance of this in order to remain open to the parenting challenge being presented are likely to be more resilient over the long term than parents who see themselves as at the bottom of the list when it comes to having support for themselves. Prioritizing the children's needs is an important quality in prospective parents, but being able to prioritize their own needs is equally important. Getting the balance between self-care and care of others is an important attribute for successful parenting.

Self-awareness is a key concept to understand as part of the assessment and preparation of prospective parents. Self-awareness will not only help the prospective parents during the assessment process, but more importantly it will help prepare them to better recognize and understand the emotional impact of relational trauma on everyone in the new family.

## Impact on parents of parenting developmentally traumatized children

Matthew is a difficult child to parent. The interactional styles that he learnt to cope with neglectful and frightening parenting early in his life and to cope with the separation and loss of these parents and his subsequent foster carers served him well. Now he is living in a permanent and safe adoptive home but his brain is wired for impermanence and danger. His attachment is insecure and disorganized. His need to stay in control means that he is not open to a reciprocal, loving relationship with his parents. At his most insecure he works hard to be self-reliant, to hide his need for comfort. This alternates, when his stress reduces, with coercive, attention-needing behaviours, demanding that his parents remain attentive to him. Neither of these styles of relating is open to a reciprocal relationship with a loving, sensitive and attuned parent. Control rather than reciprocity is the driving force of Matthew's relationships.

Belinda and Mike are Matthew's adoptive parents. They have an older birth child, Daniel, whom they have parented successfully. When parenting Daniel, his parents feel safe and competent. They enjoy being with him, but can also recover easily from times of conflict when Daniel is more oppositional. Belinda and Mike always make sure to repair their relationship with Daniel following such times, and so he experiences and can believe in unconditional love. They all enjoy reciprocal relationships in which they each have a positive influence on the other In addition, Daniel has a sense of safety and security with his parents. He has a secure attachment.

As Jonathan Baylin explores in detail in Chapter 7 and in his writing with Dan Hughes (Hughes and Baylin 2012), parenting can influence the functioning of the parental brain. This can have a devastating impact on the ability to parent a developmentally traumatized child. Understanding the impact of parenting at this biological level might be helpful in preparing and assessing prospective parents. Resilience to these impacts and the ability to use informal and professional support to recover from them will be important factors in successfully parenting developmentally traumatized children.

In the brains of parents like Belinda and Mike, when parenting Daniel their caregiving systems are switched on. They feel rewarded in the parenting task, want to approach and interact with their child and are able to tune in to his needs and make sense of his behaviours and their responses to them. They are able to provide Daniel with warmth, openness and empathy as they attune to and accept his inner life alongside providing boundaries for his behaviour and sufficient structure to help him stay safe.

With Matthew, all of these parenting abilities are challenged. Whilst they offer the same unconditional love as for Daniel, Matthew does not trust this. The structure and boundaries he experiences trigger his fears of being hurt or abandoned again and he responds with rage and terror. It is hard to enjoy being with Matthew as Belinda and Mike find themselves waiting for the next rage-filled episode. They try to attune to Matthew's needs, but his constant miscuing leaves them feeling confused and helpless. They try to give love and warmth, but it never feels like it is reciprocated. They offer nurture but Matthew rejects this in favour of his feelings of control. Neither Matthew nor Belinda and Mike feel any sense of safety and security in this relationship.

Different things happen in the brains of Belinda and Mike whilst parenting Matthew. Their caregiving systems switch off as they enter a state of blocked care (see Chapter 8). Their potential to nurture Matthew is becoming suppressed. They feel no pleasure in this relationship and find it hard to tune into his needs or to make sense of his behaviours. Parenting Matthew hurts them. They experience a painful sense of failure as parents. They feel like withdrawing. They quickly become defensive as they shout, nag and plead with him. Fortunately Belinda and Mike both have good executive functioning in their brains; the control system that allows the brain to work in an integrated state is available to them. They can think, plan and self-monitor even at their most stressed with Matthew. They are also able to seek and use the support of friends, family and professionals. This self-awareness and ability to draw on support allows them to stay present for Matthew, rather than rejecting or even hurting him back. Parenting though, has become a joyless task and they are not sure how long they can continue.

As we will explore further in Chapter 5, parents like Belinda and Mike need a particular resilience if they are to stay open and engaged in their parenting of a developmentally traumatized child like Matthew. Only then will they be able to avoid feelings of defensiveness in their parenting and continue to offer warm, nurturing care even in the face of rejecting and controlling behaviours. They will learn to understand and accept Matthew's inner life and to recognize and meet his hidden as well as his expressed needs. In this way, and with good support, they may be able to avoid or recover from blocked care and thus remain receptive and open in their parenting of him.

## Impact of early experience on capacity to parent

Earlier we explored the impact of developmental trauma on child development. This illustrated the challenges that parents will face when taking on the parenting of these children. In the previous section we highlighted the risks to parents' own caregiving systems when the child is rejecting and controlling. It is an added complication that the parents may also have their own experience of trauma, loss and being poorly parented. This will further impact upon the success of parenting developmentally traumatized children.

For example, a study of women revealed the relationship between adverse childhood experiences and adult attachment state of mind. Mothers with more adverse experiences in childhood were at greater risk of repeating those adverse experiences with their children (Murphy *et al.* 2014). The parents' previous relationship experiences will be an important factor in determining how well they can parent the developmentally traumatized child.

Mike, for example, experienced his own father leaving the family when he was an infant. His mother remarried and, although he had a reasonable relationship with his stepfather, he did experience him as rather exacting. Mike describes that he never felt he was quite good enough for him, a source of disappointment no matter how hard he tried. Now, when Matthew is rejecting or controlling, Mike can find himself taken back to this earlier, formative relationship. He experiences the same sense of failing, the same sense of being a disappointment to Matthew as he experienced with his stepfather. The suppressed anger he had but failed to acknowledge towards his stepfather now threatens to erupt in his parenting of Matthew. The relationship that Mike has with Matthew is therefore further complicated by his relationship with his stepfather.

The challenges that developmentally traumatized children display can be potent reminders of past relationship difficulties. Parents will need good self-awareness and resilience in light of these past difficulties if they are to stay present for the children. Dealing with a challenging relationship can place a strain on anyone's resources. Living with two challenging relationships in one can overwhelm even the most secure of parents.

This helps us to understand why an exploration of past relationship history, including early attachment experience, is an important part of the assessment of prospective parents. The adult attachment style that results from these relationships (researchers call this 'the attachment state of mind') will affect the way an adult engages with another in an emotionally significant relationship, such as a parent's relationship with a child. It is not so much the quality of this historical experience that is important, but how far the parents have been able to process this experience, whether good or bad. Are they able to reflect on this experience from a distance and reach an understanding of how it might have influenced the person that they have become? When they can do this, the experience is said to be integrated into their sense of self rather than cut off from it. Integration means that the parent is able to function in the present without being taken back to old struggles. They will be able to respond to the child in an attuned and sensitive way.

Lack of integration makes parents vulnerable to certain experiences with their children. For example, they may become absorbed or preoccupied with the past relationship that the children are reminding them of. Their dysregulated emotion towards people in the past becomes enacted in their parenting of their children. This preoccupation is generally unconscious; the parent experiences himself or herself as responding to the child and not to the left over feelings from their pasts. Being unaware of this influence the parents will struggle to alter or adapt their parenting responses to be attuned to the children's needs. Alternatively, the unconscious reminders might lead to a withdrawal from the affective experiences that the children are triggering within them. An emotional avoidance means the parents cannot be aware of how the children are currently feeling as they unconsciously endeavour to remain unaware of how they felt at the time of their own past experience. Again the parents in these situations will struggle to attune to the children and to respond to the need being signalled.

Assessments need to 'surprise the unconscious' so that the assessor can explore the emotional regulation of the prospective parents when reflecting upon significant past relationships as revealed in the coherence or lack of coherence in their narratives. This will help the assessor predict how the parents might respond in different parenting situations. The Adult Attachment Interview is the best known formal assessment to facilitate this type of reflection (Main *et al.* 2008). This interview is used as a research tool in the study of adult attachment states of mind, but has also influenced the questions that can be asked of parents when exploring the potential influences on current parenting (e.g. Siegel and Hartzell 2003).

When potential parents are assessed to have insecure attachment states of mind with regard to significant relationships in their history, a further assessment is needed concerning their openness to deeper reflection when supported by a skilled practitioner. This will help them to 'earn security' so that they can remain open and engaged with their future child, even when that child is triggering a defensive response within them.

Potential parents who are assessed as being unresolved for past relationship trauma trigger more concern in the assessor. Within the assessment, discussion of traumatic relationships in the past triggers more incoherence and a breakdown in the narrative that is being developed. These potential parents will need to engage in a longer period of therapy to help them integrate this past difficult experience before being reassessed for their suitability to foster or adopt.

Parenting developmentally traumatized children is a challenging task; it can take parents to places that they did not know existed as they absorb the rage, hopelessness and fear of their young children, and experience their own sense of inadequacy. It is also a rewarding task: watching a child gradually learn to trust and accept care; feeling their hand in yours for the first time; smiling when they tell you 'I love you' and mean it; watching them finally get invited to a birthday party and managing it without a meltdown! All of these small experiences can bring an exquisite satisfaction that can only be experienced when a parent has lived through the lows and hard times of parenting a child who lacks trust and rejects care. The journey is up and down, and adolescence has the parents hanging on with their fingertips again, but the small moments of success make the journey worth it.

So what happened to Matthew? Belinda and Mike found some good professional support and this, combined with good friends and some supportive family members, helped them withstand the worst times. Belinda had the hardest time as Matthew feared her love and rejected her attempts to connect to him. It was particularly tough in his early years when only she witnessed this side of him whilst to everyone else he was charm itself. At eight years of age, Matthew, with increasing developmental maturity, struggled to reconcile his experience of being adopted. He queried his role in this ('I must be a bad kid!') and longed for a birth family who would not have rejected him. The increased stress that this brought meant his anger and rage became visible to everyone. Even the smallest of boundaries and the kindest of 'no's' led to fear that he would be rejected and would lose this family too. Belinda and Mike worked with their professional supporters to understand this and to remain connected with Matthew even when he was fighting them. Most difficult for them was balancing the enormous need of their young son with those of his older brother, so that Daniel also got what he needed from his parents. With support and therapeutic help they managed however, and the pre-adolescent years were relatively calm.

There were some good family times as Matthew began to believe in what was on offer. They could not be as spontaneous as they would have liked, change and transition would always be difficult, but there was laughter and fun. Belinda treasures the photograph of Daniel and Matthew bent together over a Lego® model they were jointly constructing, a smile on each face as their heads gently touched. It was also good to see Matthew's developing friendship with Daniel, and to watch the two of them enjoying finding their feet in the wider world.

It was then seatbelt time as Matthew hit his teens. All the old doubts and fears seemed to resurface as Matthew again tried to figure out who he was and where he belonged. For a while the old Matthew was back with his need to control, reject and hate within his family. Luckily their professional support was on hand ready to mobilize and together they all figured out what was going on. Belinda and Mike revisited old strategies. They would creep into Matthew's bedroom at night to watch him sleeping and remember the love they would always have for their child. A therapist worked with them all so that Matthew could experience his parents' acceptance and understanding of his biggest rages and worst fears.

Matthew discovered his own identity as adopted child, son and brother, and the trust that had begun to develop in childhood was strengthened in his later adolescence. Matthew left home when he was ready, which was in his mid-20s. He came back often, sharing with them his success as an engineer. As he approached 30 he found a steady partnership with Ruth. The proudest moment of Belinda and Mike's life was watching Matthew hold his small infant son. As they watched the two gaze at each other they knew that, despite the ups and downs, they had got there and that their son no longer had to carry the legacy of his earliest days.

---

### BOX 2.2 HOW UNDERSTANDING THE IMPACT OF DEVELOPMENTAL TRAUMA CAN INFLUENCE THE ASSESSMENT PROCESS

Assessors need an understanding of:

- the experience of the children
- the impact of this experience on development
- the parenting challenges that this can present.

This will inform the assessment of whether the potential parents will be able to *understand the experience of the child*. Can they:

- relate understanding to current behaviours even when these are complex, challenging and perplexing
- recognize the impact of understanding this experience upon themselves and other family members
- recognize the impact of living with this understanding and the resulting behaviours on themselves and other family members
- be open to support from skilled practitioners who can join with them in making sense of the children
- have the emotional resources to retain this understanding under stress?

Assessment will need to consider whether parents are likely to be *flexible and adaptable*. Are they likely to:

- have flexibility in their attitudes about how to parent children
- be prepared to adjust parenting to take into account the impact of early experience on the child
- have flexibility and adaptability in the face of challenges presented by the child?

Ability to *look after self and family* will be an important part of the assessment. Are they likely to:

- recognize when emotional resources are running dry
- be able to prioritize themselves and use self-care when it is needed
- be able to balance the child's needs with their own self-care needs and those of all the family
- be open to support from others when taking care of themselves?

Finally assessment will also encompass *self-awareness in understanding past experience and the potential impact on themselves as parents*. Are they:

- open to reflecting on past relationship experience
- able to provide a coherent narrative and stay emotionally regulated when reflecting on difficult experience
- able to be open to recognizing potential vulnerabilities and to be supported to explore this further
- prepared to undergo therapy when past relationship trauma is unresolved, thus slowing down the assessment process with the need for reassessment following conclusion of the therapy?

## Conclusion

A child who has experienced developmental trauma can pose a particular challenge to those who later come to parent him. By its very nature this type of complex trauma beginning early in the child's life can have a large impact on subsequent development. The range of influences that this can have on attachment, behaviour, emotional regulation, cognition and identity can mean that parenting the child is complex. The parent can find that the child has an impact upon them that is unexpected, rocking the very foundations of who they imagined themselves to be as parents. This impact is at a biological as well as a behavioural level, having surprising effects on the brain as well as on the body. Blocked care is a very real danger when parenting a child whose capacity to trust is also blocked (see Chapter 8).

Assessment of prospective parents will need to be mindful of the impact of developmental trauma upon the child and the particular parenting challenges that this presents. A parent's ability to be understanding, flexible and responsive will be important. Regulation and reflection under stress will need to be explored. Resilience and willingness to accept support will equally be important qualities the prospective parent will need when taking on the long-term task of parenting a child with experience of developmental trauma.

# References

Briere, J. N. (2002) 'Treating adult survivors of severe childhood abuse and neglect: Further developments of an integrative model.' In J. E. B. Myers, L. Berliner, J. Briere, C. T. Hendrix, C. Jenny and T. A. Reid (eds) *The APSAC Handbook on Child Maltreatment, 2nd edition*. London: Sage Publications.

Briere, J. N. and Scott, C. (2006) *Principles of Trauma Therapy: A Guide to Symptoms, Evaluation, and Treatment*. London: Sage Publications.

Cook, A., Spinazzola, J., Ford, J., Lanktree, C., Balustein, M., Sprague, C. *et al.* (2005) 'Complex trauma in children and adolescents.' *Psychiatric Annals 35*, 5, 390–398.

Fairbank, J. A. (2008) 'The epidemiology of trauma and trauma related disorders in children and youth.' *PTSD Research Quarterly 19*, 1, 1050–1835.

Hughes, D. A. and Baylin, J. (2012) *Brain-based Parenting: The Neuroscience of Caregiving for Healthy Attachment*. New York: W.W. Norton.

Main, M., Goldwyn, R. and Hesse, E. (2008) 'The Adult Attachment Interview, scoring and classification system, version 8.' Unpublished manuscript. Berkeley: University of California.

Murphy, A., Steele, M., Dube, S. R., Bate, J., Bonuck, K., Meissner, P., Goldman, H. and Steele H. (2014) 'Adverse childhood experiences (ACEs) questionnaire and adult attachment interview (AAI): Implications for parent child relationships.' *Child Abuse and Neglect 38*, 2, 224–233.

Perry, B. D. (2002) 'Childhood experience and the expression of genetic potential: What childhood neglect tells us about nature and nurture.' *Brain and Mind 3*, 79–100.

Siegel, D. J. and Hartzell, M. (2003) *Parenting from the Inside Out*. New York: Tarcher/Putnam.

van der Kolk, B. (2005) 'Developmental trauma disorder. Towards a rational diagnosis for children with complex trauma histories.' *Psychiatric Annals 5*, 401–408.

# CHAPTER 3

# The Home Study and Assessment of Applicants

## Research Evidence

*Julie Selwyn*

In most countries, the only eligibility criteria stipulated in law for those wanting to become adoptive parents are the applicants' age, good health, a residency requirement and a lack of criminal offences. Assessments are therefore guided by many factors including historical practices, cultural and religious views, practice guidance, child development theory and research. Given the importance of the assessment for the approval of prospective adoptive parents and for later matching and support plans, it is surprising that there is so little research on home studies (Crea, Barth and Chintapalli 2007). Yet inspections, social work professionals, prospective adoptive parents and researchers (e.g. Social Services Inspectorate 1993; O'Sullivan 2004; Adoption UK 2011; Department for Education (DfE) 2011) have repeatedly raised concerns about the content and the process of assessment.

In this chapter, we begin by considering concerns about the variability and accuracy of assessments and three models that have been developed to try to address those concerns. In the second half of the chapter, three specific but interlinked elements of the assessment are examined: parental expectations, parental sensitivity and the management of stress.

*The home study* has to evaluate the suitability of the applicants to become adoptive parents, but it also has a number of other functions. It provides the opportunity for the prospective adopters to explore their own concerns, for discussion and reflection on the realities of adoption, and for the applicants and the social worker to get to know each other, so that later the best match can be made. As prospective adopters become more knowledgeable about adoption and reflect on their own capacities, original preferences and views often change. The assessment task is complex, as expectations, preferences and capacities are not fixed but dynamic, responding to the changes in the environment. Adding to the complexity of the home study is that often applicants have no previous experience of parenting and, therefore, judgements are being made about *potential* rather than what can be observed. The final assessment document has many uses: it is the key evidence on which the approval is based and it provides the information to aid with matching and the development of the support plan once the child/ren are placed.

Assessing adoptive applicants is a skilled task. Many hours are spent preparing and writing the home study. In England, research has estimated that reports take on average 74 social work hours to complete (Selwyn *et al.* 2006) but this can vary depending on the complexity of the case from 24 to 170 hours (Dance *et al.* 2010). The social work role is complex, being friend, mentor, educator, assessor and the shaper of expectations. Inevitably, this can produce role conflicts particularly when applicants might need to be counselled out or when the recommendation is that the applicant(s) are unsuitable (Selwyn 1994; Geen, Malm and Katz 2004; Wilson, Kahn and Geen 2005).

## Indicators for selection

While there has been a great deal of research examining the assessment of parenting in high risk groups such as those subject to a child protection investigation (Reder, Duncan and Lucey 2003; Jones 2009; Turney *et al.* 2012), there has been far less research on the assessment of adoptive parents. Rushton's (2003) review of adoption research found that:

> Various parent characteristics have been proposed and are currently used as good indicators for selection of prospective adopters: child centredness, warmth, consistency, flexibility, tenacity, a sense of humour, capacity to reflect on problems and their origins and inventiveness in parenting strategies. However, no evidence has been gathered that possession of any of these characteristics independently predicts a successful placement. It is likely that a complex interaction of factors is responsible for which placements disrupt and which survive satisfactorily. To date, no studies have collected data at the point of assessment and related it to placement outcome. (Rushton 2003, p.8)

In addition to the characteristics required of any parent, research has emphasized the importance of applicants having: (1) realistic expectations; (2) a stable marriage/relationship; (3) open communication; (4) flexibility and tolerance; (5) successful resolutions of previous trauma/losses; (6) tenacity; and (7) a sense of humour (Brodzinsky 2008; Benzies and Mychasiuk 2009). Quinton's (2012) review of matching in adoptions from care quotes the Donaldson Institute's review (2004), which highlighted the following as the characteristics of successful adoptive parents:

> Commitment; a flexible and relaxed approach to parenting; realistic expectations; and an ability to distance themselves from the child's behaviour; and a willingness to work with the agency and to understand that the information about the child is related to success. (p.95)

Quinton (2012) noted that while there is general agreement about the sought after characteristics it would be unlikely for an applicant to have all of them. Nor do we know whether some characteristics are more important than others and whether the presence/absence of some characteristics should carry greater weight when matching to children with specific behaviours or difficulties.

## Concerns about assessments

In most UK studies of domestic adoption (e.g. Lowe *et al.* 1999; Selwyn *et al.* 2006), parents generally report satisfaction with the assessment process. Some parents state that they appreciated being given the opportunity to reflect on their lives, whereas other parents saw it as a necessary hurdle that had to be overcome to reach their goal. A smaller proportion of parents reported that they disliked the assessment process. In a study of adoptive parents who had adopted three or more siblings, one of the motivating factors for taking a large sibling group was to avoid having to go through the assessment process again (Saunders and Selwyn 2011).

The kinds of complaints made by adoptive parents about their assessments are consistent across studies and surveys (Wilson *et al.* 2005; DfE 2011; Harding 2012; Birmingham City Council 2012). Prospective adopters complain about the purpose and content of an assessment not being explained, being subjected to assessments with no clear timeframes, and too great a focus on health and safety, or on 'ticking boxes'. Other complaints are of a lack of clarity about whether the preparation groups are part of the assessment, why certain information is gathered, and how it will be used. Adopters report they have felt unable to complain about delays or poor service, because they feared that it might affect their chances of adopting a child (Expert Working Group on Adoption 2012).

## Concerns about variable quality and lack of analysis

In the UK, professionals have complained that assessment documents can contain lengthy description but little analysis (DfE 2011). Similar complaints about the lack of analysis in other kinds of social work assessments have been reported elsewhere (Munro 2011; Turney *et al.* 2012). However, lack of analysis and variable quality in adopter assessments are not just an issue for the UK, but have been reported in other countries such as the US (e.g. Crea *et al.* 2007) and the Netherlands (e.g. Stroobants, Vanderfaille and Put 2011).

In many countries, applicants are asked to write an autobiography – the story of their life – and this forms a central component of the home study. Noordegraaf, van Nijnatten and Elbers (2009a, 2009b) investigated the accuracy and thoroughness of autobiographies, as a reflection of the applicants' level of functioning. The study found that prospective adopters created a story of 'normality' in terms of their background and experiences. Workers too, often failed to identify and ignored or downplayed possible risks. There was a tendency for workers to search for what they expected to find and to ignore any contradictory information. In summary, research in the US and the Netherlands found that home study reports were often limited to verbatim reporting of information that the family had provided and lacked a critical analysis of family functioning related to parenting ability and readiness (Crea *et al.* 2007; Stroobants *et al.* 2011).

In the US, some agencies have used a mutual strength-based assessment approach to writing the home study report. There has been a merger of preparation and assessment. However, researchers in the US (Crea *et al.* 2007, 2009b) point out that such an approach is inappropriate, as it depends on knowledgeable, accurate and truthful disclosure by applicants of relevant family information. Unfortunately, families are often either innocently unable or actively unwilling to provide truthful information. Families want to manage how they are perceived by social workers (Geen *et al.* 2004). Consequently, social workers need to retain their power to screen out prospective adopters who may pose a risk to children, or those whose motivation is not child centred (see, for example, the serious case review on the death of John Smith placed for adoption in the UK[1]).

## Models of assessment

To overcome the identified difficulties there have been attempts in the UK, US and the Netherlands to make the home study more relevant, consistent and structured.

## UK

In the UK, all agencies use the parenting assessment record (PAR) developed by the British Association of Adoption and Fostering (BAAF). The PAR requires social workers to collect information on the applicants' personal details, personality and interests, experience and lifestyle, support networks and type of placement offered. The completed report is expected to include a family tree, an ecomap and a chronology. Applicants can read the final assessment report and have the opportunity to write their own comments on the social worker's report. The PAR should be completed within four months and the report contains separate sections on the following areas:

- family background and early experience including education
- adult life – work, health and other issues
- relationships and support networks
- the home, financial circumstances and lifestyle
- motivation to adopt and expectations of placement
- understanding of the needs of adopted children and adoptive parenting capacity.

The PAR closely follows the advice in the DfE government guidance on 'Preparing and Assessing Adopters' (DfE 2006) and there are additional assessment resources, training guides and DVDs published by BAAF (e.g. Beesley 2010; Dibben 2010; Cousins 2010). DfE guidance recommends the use of several standardized measures such as the Home Inventory and the Family Pack of Questionnaires.[2] However, a survey (Dance *et al.* 2010) of English agencies found that only a few agencies used the Home Inventory and social workers rarely made use of any standardized measures to aid assessments or evaluate their work.

Although all agencies use the PAR there is variation between and within agencies on the emphases and weight placed on psychological exploration, information collecting and preparation. For example, Dance and colleagues' survey (2010) of agency practice found that some agencies required applicants to keep a 'learning log' during the assessment and preparation period. The log was used to record adopters' learning experiences and provided a way that they could evidence their capacity for critical reflection (Moon 2004). Indeed some agencies[3] emphasize the capacity for reflective thinking and emotional openness as key assessment criteria.

The PAR was revised in 2013 in response to criticisms that assessment reports were overly long and descriptive with little analysis. The new PAR places more emphasis on the analysis of relevant information. However, other than stating that analysis is required and leaving space on the form for the analysis to be inserted, there is no structure to aid analysis.

## STRUCTURED INTERVIEWS

In a few English adoption agencies the PAR is supplemented with one of two structured interviews: the Adult Attachment Interview (AAI; Steele *et al.* 2000) or The Attachment Style Interview for Adoption and Fostering (ASI-AF) (Bifulco *et al.* 2008).

The *AAI* asks about applicants' childhood experiences, including times when they were hurt, ill or tired, and their memories of parental discipline, separations and rejection. Instead of accepting reports of childhood experience at face value, the AAI uses qualitative features of the adult's narrative to anchor and evaluate adults' self-reports. Based on the coherence and balance of the adult's narrative a rating of attachment classification (secure, insecure avoidant/dismissive, insecure enmeshed, unresolved) is made by the interviewer. The rating indicates the internalized images of parental relationships the adopters are bringing to their role as parents. The AAI has been used and validated in many research studies (e.g. van IJzendoorn 1995) but is used by only a few adoption agency staff in England when assessing prospective adopters.

The *ASI-AF* has a focus on current close relationships, the capacity to access and use support, as well as attachment styles (enmeshed, fearful, angry-dismissive, withdrawn, and secure). For example, questions in the interviews are: Can you describe a recent problem that you confided in your partner? How often do you have arguments or rows? How would you feel if your friend moved away to live?

Workers need to be trained before they can use the AAI and ASI-AF, and agencies have been reluctant to invest because of the training costs, the fact that they can be difficult to interpret (Farnfield 2008), and because additional worker time is needed to transcribe and rate each interview. Workers report that they like both types of interview but as yet there is no evidence for their role in matching or predictive capability (Quinton 2012). However, there are indications that the structured interviews could identify adopters who need interventions prior to placement and flag up the families who would be more vulnerable to stress (Kanuik, Steele and Hodges 2004).

## US

In the US, there are a number of assessment models that cover similar ground to the PAR (e.g. the Ohio Family Interview Guide[4] and Child Welfare Information Gateway 2010). One of the most widely used models is Structured Analysis Family Evaluation (SAFE; Consortium SAFE 2011), which has an evidence base and is the only known home study approach with an ongoing research programme. SAFE[5] is more structured than the British PAR and is currently used in half of US states and six Canadian provinces (Crea *et al.* 2007, 2009b). It was developed to consider the strengths and skills required to parent adopted, fostered and kinship children, and to create a comprehensive and uniform instrument to gather prospective family information including an in-depth psychosocial evaluation. It was also designed to reduce variability and to ensure that difficult topics were discussed (Crea *et al.* 2011). It was not intended to replace preparation group training programmes.

In the SAFE model, prior to being interviewed, all applicants complete a questionnaire to ensure that every applicant is asked, and every worker considers, *all* core home study questions in *every* case. For example, there are questions on who parented the applicant and experiences of early separation. The intention is that workers do not miss, either consciously or unconsciously, areas that they find personally difficult. The questionnaire responses are then used by the social worker to determine which issues require further clarification and which should be the focus of the home study interviews. Although SAFE is structured, it still relies on social work skills to encourage and enable prospective parents to tell their story and to probe areas of concern. During the home study, a second questionnaire is completed by the worker and applicants together on areas such as alcohol and drug misuse and stressful life experiences. The focused interview itself covers 62 psycho-social factors, which are grouped into nine sections, and these are rated several times over the course of the home study on a Likert type scale of 1–5: a rating of 1 being of no concern and 5 being of serious concern. All the information is collated and there is a desk-based tool to help the social worker rate and analyse the information. This process is guided by explicit analytical components that are intended to produce a clear decision as to whether an identified concern remains, is reduced or no longer exists. These components include: (1) the actual area of concern; (2) its extent, frequency and severity; (3) its roots in time, place and context; (4) the applicant's degree of resolution or adaptation; (5) the strength of the applicant's resolution or adaptation; (6) the amount of energy required to sustain the resolution or adaptation; and (7) a statement of the evidence that supports this evaluation. The final ratings along with an informed social work judgement are applied to any of the psychosocial inventory factors that were rated as 'issues of concern'.

As with the PAR, the final report is formatted so that there is consistency in the presentation of the assessment, and prospective adopters are required to review and sign the home study. Finally, the SAFE model includes a matching inventory, a structured compatibility list designed to assist placement workers in assessing the 'goodness of fit' between children and prospective families.

Research examining social workers' experiences with the implementation of SAFE (Crea *et al.* 2009a, 2009b) found that it more effectively identified issues of concern (such as alcohol misuse) when compared with conventional methods. Practitioners also thought it was fairer, more thorough and most preferred it. However, SAFE was more favourably reviewed by new and less experienced social workers who liked the structure of SAFE. More experienced workers disliked the lack of discretion, missed the autobiographical interview and thought that the quality of the assessment was determined by the skills of the worker. Ongoing longitudinal research examining outcomes where SAFE has been used in comparison with other methods will provide more evidence.

## The Netherlands

Unlike the UK, the vast majority of adoptions in the Netherlands are inter-country adoptions. Domestic adoptions are rare, only about 40 a year (Vinke 2008). Until the late 1990s, prospective adoptive parents had to be younger than 42 years old and children no older than six years old when they arrived in the Netherlands. In recent years, there has been a slight relaxation of the applicants' age requirements. Adopters can now be aged up to 46 years old if they are taking an older child or a child with special needs. In comparison, the UK has no upper age limit for prospective adopters, although there is an expectation that the adults' expected life span would enable them to see the child into adulthood.

Assessments in the Netherlands are conducted by child protection board social workers, who have all had specific training in adoption-related issues. The social workers are based in multi-disciplinary teams enabling additional interviews or separate psychological evaluations to be readily undertaken if necessary. The assessment is expected to be completed in three and a half months. There are four key documents. First the Home Study Manual and the home study report (Smulders and van Tuyll 2003/2004), and two manuals, one with instructions on background material for screening and a specialized manual for the assessment of those adopting a child with special needs (Groenhuijsen 2009).

A framework of risk and protective factors (Stroobants *et al.* 2011; Vinke 2013) informed by research guides the assessment process. The framework was developed by Vinke (1999; 2013) using a model of child development based on the work of Belsky, Robbins and Gamble (1984) and Rispens, Goudena and Groenendaal (1994) and incorporating the additional developmental tasks associated with adoption. It takes an ecological perspective, examining risks and protective factors in the parents, family and the environment.

As in the UK and US, the intention behind the framework is to make decision making more transparent and well documented. The elements in the framework – parent's characteristics, motivations, personality and skills, their beliefs and expectations about adoptive parenting and the child, life events, marital relationship, response to childlessness/loss, and family and environmental characteristics

– would be familiar to most social workers. However, the difference lies in the emphasis on the identification of risk and protective factors for each of the elements. The framework provides guidance on the factors that should be considered. For example, in assessing the applicants' beliefs about a future adopted child a social worker is expected to assess:

> Protective factors: an ability to adjust expectations, cope with the child's history and an ability to help the child cope with the facts, differences are acknowledged and taken into account.

> Risk factors: a belief that the child can replace a dreamt of biological child, having an expectation of gratitude or expecting immediate unconditional attachment, an attitude of rejecting difference leaving little room for the child to become their own person.

Adoptive parents over the age of 42 years old have an additional set of five questionnaire measures to complete. The questionnaires measure psychological health (SLC-90; Derogatis, Lipman and Covi 1973), coping style (Utrecht coping list; Schreurs, Tellegen and van der Willige 1984), personality (Dutch Personality Questionnaire; Luteirjn, Starren and VanDijk 2000), problem solving (IPOV; Lange 1983), and there is an adoption-specific questionnaire (Vinke and Van Tuyll 1996). The measures are scored and interpreted by a psychologist and a profile is created of the risk and protective factors. An evaluation (Stroobants *et al.* 2011) of the use of the measures found that the rejection rate of applicants increased by 0.5 per cent to 7 per cent. If withdrawals were taken into account the overall rejection rate increased to 25 per cent.

The social worker conducts the first home interview and, later, her/his impressions and findings are compared with the profile and discussed in the multi-disciplinary team. The rest of the assessment procedure is shaped according to the issues raised during the discussion.

In all three countries, there have been concerns about the quality of assessment especially the dominance of descriptive rather than analytical content, avoidance of difficult issues and judgements of suitability not rooted in evidence but worker bias. The US and the Netherlands have developed more structured assessments and a greater reliance on standardized questionnaire measures compared to the UK. In comparison with the UK, workers in those countries seem to be more willing to ask for, and have access to an independent psychological assessment if the assessing social worker has concerns and/or for assessments to be conducted by multi-disciplinary teams.

However, we do not know whether selection has improved as a result of the changes in the three countries. It is clear that whatever model is used, the skill of the social worker in shaping expectations, working with the applicants in enabling them to consider their capacities, drawing out the issues of concern and analysing a mass of sometimes contradictory information remains fundamental to the assessment task.

In the next section, the focus is on three areas that assessments need to examine: (1) parental hopes and expectations; (2) parental sensitivity; and (3) management of stress and support networks.

## Hopes and expectations

Evidence suggests that parents who have unrealistic or developmentally inappropriate expectations are more likely to be dissatisfied with adoption and to have a difficult relationship with their adopted child (e.g. Barth and Berry 1988; Sar 2000). For example, parents will be dissatisfied if they have expectations of academic achievement higher than the child's abilities. Conversely, realistic expectations are associated with higher parental satisfaction and greater child self-esteem (Brodzinsky and Schecter 1990; Reilly and Platz 2003).

Expectations are a difficult area to assess (see Gray 2007) as social workers have a major role in shaping parental expectation through the information they provide on the children available for adoption. In the UK, there is a significant gap in knowledge about the long-term outcomes of maltreated children placed for adoption from the care system. Emerging evidence is of rates of autistic type behaviours (Green *et al.* in press), learning difficulties and mental health problems (Biehal *et al.* 2010; Selwyn, Wijedasa and Meakings 2014) being much higher in children adopted out of care than would be expected in the general population. Of course, children's challenging behaviour can and does improve but persistence is the message from research.

In our studies (Selwyn *et al.* 2006, 2014) of adoptive family life, some parents' expectations had been shaped by social workers who had been overly optimistic about what could be achieved with stability, love and the resources at many adoptive parents' disposal. Parents did not have high expectations of academic achievement but they did hope to create a family that resembled the one of their dreams. Some mothers stated that they had hoped that they could have the same close relationship with their adoptive child as they had had with their own mother. Parents' beliefs of what a 'mother' or 'father' should be like, were not what their adoptive child was willing to accept. Adopters said:

> He's had a lot of different mothers along the way. And I'm one of them and I'm the one that's still there. I'm the one that's got the cheque book and a purse and remembers birthdays and Christmases. I'm not the mum he would like to have…his concept [of being a mum] is different.

Reflecting on their original hopes and expectations, parents said of their experience of adopting looked-after children:

> You might have all this love, but they don't want it. You have to find a different way.

> Thinking that all these lovely experiences meant that they were going to grow up like normal children.

> The worst part of it all is seeing them struggle with things that an ordinary child from a normal family would do and knowing that this family is not normal and it never will be and never could be. But I didn't know that would be a possibility when I adopted them.

Over time, some of the adoptive parents said they had learnt to accept children for who they were and to stop blaming themselves for lack of improvement. They had learnt to take pleasure in small things.

Reder, Duncan and Gray (1993) drew attention to understanding the meaning of the child in families where a child had died because of maltreatment. Assessments of prospective adopters must also consider the meaning of the child for the applicants and what adopters expect from family life. Expectations are not simply about unrealistic academic achievements but capacity to accept a very different kind of family life than that envisaged. Questions need to be asked such as, how would the applicants feel if the child never called them mum and dad? Would they be able to go at the child's pace and not force intimacy? This requires parents who are sensitive to the child and who can see and feel things from a child's point of view.

## Sensitivity and warmth

In her description of sensitive mothers, Mary Ainsworth (1982) focused on maternal behaviours such as sensitivity to the child's signals, interpreting the signals correctly and responding appropriately and promptly. She also noted that maternal sensitivity was dependent on being able to empathize with the infant and having insight into one's own moods and wishes. Ainsworth argued that these internal processes led to a more realistic judgement of the child's behaviour, probably because it allowed the mother to separate her own feelings from the infant's signals.

Research has found that insightful mothers are more likely to have securely attached children. This finding has been replicated in general population samples and in samples of children with difficulties on the autistic spectrum, with foster children and those with learning difficulties (Oppenheim and Koren-Karie 2013). Sensitivity can be assessed using a range of tools (e.g. see review by Mesman and Emmen 2013, Ainsworth Scales and the insightfulness assessment, Oppenheim and Koren-Karie 2013).

There is also substantial evidence that being able to express warmth and love is associated with closer child–parent relationships (Zeanah, Berlin and Boris 2011). However, looked-after children may have very weak signals and/or be avoidant of comfort. Difficulties with intimacy and trust often go unrecognized in foster care, although there are interventions that promote sensitive adoptive and foster parenting (e.g. Schofield and Beek 2006; Dozier *et al.* 2009; Juffer, Bakermans-Kranenburg and van Ijzendoorn 2008; Leve *et al.* 2012).

Ainsworth's attention to internal processes and what would now be termed mentalization or mind-mindedness (Fonagy *et al.* 1995;

Meins *et al.* 2013) has gained greater prominence in recent years. Reflective functioning (RF) has been described as the verbal expression of the internal mentalizing capacity (Slade 2005). Fonagy and colleagues (1998) assessed RF by adding a scale to the AAI to examine adults' capacity to reflect and consider mental states in their own parents, for example, by asking questions such as 'Why do you think your parents behaved in the way they did?' Parents whose AAIs were rated as high in RF were themselves likely to be classified as secure and to have children who were also securely attached (Fonagy *et al.* 1995).

Research (Fonagy *et al.* 1991) has examined how adults who were able to process early traumatic experiences in a reflective way were far less likely to develop personality disorders than adults without the capacity to reflect. RF, it is argued, appears to serve both protective and mediating functions in the development of psychopathology (Slade 2005). Adoption research has also found an association between prospective parents' lack of maternal sensitivity, their internalized representations of attachment and the risk of poor adoption outcomes (e.g. McRoy 1999; Steele 2003; Kaniuk *et al.* 2004; Beijersbergen *et al.* 2012).

AAI narratives refer to relationships during *childhood.* However, assessment of RF is sometimes more concerned with the parent's *current* relationship with their own child and capacity to keep that child in mind. Assessments of RF in current relationships usually use the Parent Development Interview (Aber *et al.* 1985; Slade 2004) or the Working model of the Child Interview (Benoit, Parker and Zeanah 1997). The Parent Development Interview has been adapted for use with adoptive and foster parents (Steele 2003).

Bowlby (1969) believed that the adult attachment style remains linked to the psychological and biological systems that regulate threat appraisal, stress response and recovery from stress. Research is beginning to show a link between adult attachment style and response to stress (e.g. Kidd, Hamer and Steptoe 2011). Those applying to become adoptive parents should expect to experience increased stress in a number of ways.

## Stress

First, there is the normative stress of becoming a new parent or of adding an additional child or children to the family. The adoption process itself is also stressful and can be exacerbated by difficult introductions and/or a difficult transition for the child from foster care to the adoptive home. Stress may also occur because of challenging child behaviours, difficulty in accessing support, negative reactions from others in the community to adoption, resurrected feelings related to prior losses (e.g. infertility) or the child's presence or behaviour placing pressure on the marital/family relationships. All of these sources of increased stress can have an impact upon the parent's ability to perceive and respond to the child's attachment signals, leading to the use of poorer parenting strategies (Lipscombe, Moyers and Farmer 2004) and lower levels of parental satisfaction with the adoption (Mainemer, Gilman and Ames 1998; Hoksbergen et al. 2004; Rijk et al. 2006).

Whether stress becomes harmful depends on the balance between appraised demands and appraised resources. On the demand side will be factors such as the intensity of the stressful event, number of events and the parent's perception of the consequences of failing to deal with the event. On the resource side will be the parent's perceptions of the resources available within the family network and the accessibility and appropriateness of professional support services, as well as perceptions of how a request for help might be viewed. For example, adoptive parents often report that they fear being viewed as inadequate or failing parents if they ask for help. The fear is not without foundation, as some adoptive parents report that they have felt blamed by professionals for child behaviours that were evident before the child was placed (Selwyn et al. 2014).

It has been argued that any individual stressful event is a poor predictor of how a person will respond to future events. Measurement of *coping resources* will be more predictive of stressful reactions than will be measurement of demands (Hobfoll 1988). Yet most measures of stress assess coping responses (i.e. behaviours that occur as a result of stress) rather than coping resources, which are factors in place *before* stressors occur (Wheaton 1983).

One of the most commonly used resource questionnaire measures is the coping resource inventory (CRIS) (Matheny *et al.* 1987, 2003). CRIS asks about behaviours, attitudes, feelings and beliefs in a number of areas including the extent to which a person is free from financial stress and health problems and has an *available* network of family and friends. In addition, CRIS also asks about personal characteristics such as how accepting a person is of their own shortcomings, whether they have a need to be liked and their willingness to disclose feelings and troubles, as well as their awareness of when tension is building up in the body and their use of exercise, thought processes and relaxation to manage stress.

The areas identified in CRIS are useful to consider in adopter assessments but they are situation dependent. For example, CRIS asks about assertiveness and a sample statement from the inventory is, 'I am very good at standing up for my rights.' Assertiveness may not be apparent at the time of the assessment, as many parents in our studies (Selwyn *et al.* 2006, 2014) stated that they had amazed themselves at their capacity to fight and argue with professionals for resources for their child. One mother reflecting on how she and her husband had been changed by her adoption experiences said:

> We were very quiet…I wouldn't have said boo to a goose. I certainly wouldn't have argued with a professional.

There is also an assumption in the coping and stress questionnaires that the resources to manage stress will be primarily internal. However, given the challenging behaviour of some adopted children, parents need to be able to draw on support from a range of professionals and agencies.

## Support networks

Research on resilience and maltreated children shows the importance of the supports around the child in enabling recovery and development. The greater the adversity the child has experienced the fewer internal resources the child can rely on and the more important the external supports become (Cicchetti 2013; Ungar, Ghazinour and Richter 2013).

All home studies ask about the support of family and friends and the likely support the prospective adopters can expect. It is sometimes assumed that the more family and community support available, the better. However, our research (Selwyn *et al.* 2006, 2014) has found that support from family and friends often melts away when children's behaviour becomes challenging. Foster care research has also found that family and friends can also be a source of stress and can be hostile and critical (Farmer, Moyers and Lipscombe 2004; Sinclair, Gibbs and Wilson 2004).

Therefore, home studies must assess the available external supports. For example, assessments should consider the available support in local schools for children with special needs, whether there are specialized services for children with difficulties on the autistic spectrum, the availability and access to child and adolescent mental health services, and whether there are appropriate services for children who have been sexually abused or those with attachment difficulties. If children's challenging behaviour is very demanding and support and services are unavailable, stress will ensue and children's outcomes are likely to be poorer. Many home assessments do not examine the environmental context, although it is recognized that adopted children are likely to need support at some point in their lives. Applicants could be asked to find out about services in their own communities and identify strengths and gaps in provision, as part of their assessment. A greater focus on assessing the environment might also get the message across to adoptive parents that they can ask for help.

## Conclusion

Assessing prospective adoptive parents is a complex task. Current best practice in assessment is seen as requiring a combination of approaches including interviews, observation, psychological tools and reports. The capacity to parent is determined by a range of psychosocial factors but that capacity is not fixed. Parenting capacity undergoes constant change depending on the circumstances facing parents and their children at any given moment in time, and the resources available to meet those challenges.

Models, other than the PAR, need testing out in the UK and more research is needed on whether certain characteristics should be preferentially weighted. Similarly, more psychological input to assessments should be encouraged.

Yet only so much can be gained from the pre-placement assessment, as much depends on the interaction of the parent with their child or children. While assessments of parents are detailed, there is often far less attention paid to assessments of children waiting to be adopted. Even good child assessments are unable to predict with accuracy those children who will develop mental health problems in adolescence. It then becomes particularly important for adoption workers to be able to detect the first signs of relationships running into difficulty and provide support to families in a non-judgemental way.

## Endnotes

1. See www.lgcplus.com/death-of-john-anthony-smith-council-statement-independent-review-conclusions-and-agencies-response/1317355.article.

2. The pack includes Parenting Daily Hassles, Family Activity Scales, Alcohol use, Recent life events, available at www.teescpp.org.uk/Websites/safeguarding/images/Documents/Family-pack-of-scales-and-questionnaires.pdf.

3. For example, http://leedschildcare.proceduresonline.com/chapters/g_criteria_assess.html.

4. See www.ocwtp.net/PDFs/Trainee%20Resources/Assessor%20Resources/FAMILY%20INTERVIEW%20GUIDE.pdf.

5. See an example at http://calswec.berkeley.edu/sites/default/files/uploads/seg06_ho15_structured_analysis_family_evaluation.pdf and at www.safehomestudy.org and at www.safehomestudy.org.

## References

Aber J. L., Slade A., Berger B., Bresgi, I. and Kaplan M. (1985) *The Parent Development Interview.* Unpublished manuscript.

Adoption UK (2011) *Supporting adopters.* Available at www.adoptionuk.org/sites/default/files/documents/SupportingAdopters-AdoptionUKspolicyrecommendations2011.pdf, accessed on 7 November 2014.

Ainsworth, M. D. S. (n.d.) *Maternal sensitivity scales.* Available at www.psychology. sunysb.edu/attachment/measures/content/ainsworth scales.html, accessed on 7 November 2014.

Ainsworth M. D. S. (1982) 'Attachment: Retrospect and Prospect.' In C. M. Parkes and J. Stevenson-Hinde (eds) *The Place of Attachment in Human Behaviour.* New York: Basic Books.

Barth, R. P. and Berry, M. (1988) *Adoption and Disruption: Rates, Risks, and Responses.* Hawthorne, NY: Aldine de Gruyter.

Beesley, P. (2010) *Making Good Assessments: A Practical Resource Guide.* London: BAAF.

Beijersbergen, M. D., Juffer, F., Bakermans-Kranenburg, M. J. and Van IJzendoorn, M. H. (2012) 'Remaining or becoming secure: Parental sensitive support predicts attachment continuity from infancy to adolescence in a longitudinal adoption study.' *Developmental Psychology 48,* 5, 1277–1282.

Belsky, J., Robbins, E. and Gamble, W. (1984) 'The Determinants of Parental Competence: Towards a Contextual Theory.' In M. Lewis and L. Rosenblum (eds) *Social Connections: Beyond the Dyad,* New York: Plenum Press.

Benzies, K. and Mychasiuk, R. (2009) 'Fostering family resiliency: A review of the key protective factors.' *Child and Family Social Work 14,* 1, 103–114.

Benoit, D., Parker, K. and Zeanah, C. (1997) 'Mothers' representations of their infant assessed prenatally: Stability and association with their infants' attachment classification.' *Journal of Consulting and Clinical Psychology 38,* 307–313.

Biehal, N., Ellison, S., Baker, C. and Sinclair, I. (2010) *Belonging and Permanence: Outcomes in Long-Term Foster Care and Adoption.* London: BAAF.

Bifulco, A., Jacobs, C., Bunn, A., Thomas, G. and Irving, K. (2008) 'The Attachment Interview (ASI) as an assessment of support capacity.' *Adoption and Fostering 32,* 33–45.

Birmingham City Council (2012) *The customers' story.* Available at www. westmidlandsiep.gov.uk/storage/resources/documents/Adoption_Customer_ Research_21_12_2012_%281%29.pdf, accessed on 16 March 2015.

Bowlby, J. (1969) *Attachment and Loss: Volume 1.* New York: Basic Books.

Brodzinsky, D. M. (2008) *Adoptive Parent Preparation Project. Phase I: Meeting the Mental Health and Developmental Needs of Adopted Children.* New York: Evan B. Donaldson Adoption Institute.

Brodzinsky, D. M. and Schechter, M. D. (eds) (1990) *The Psychology of Adoption.* New York: Oxford University Press.

Child Welfare Information Gateway (2010) *The adoption home study process.* Available at www.childwelfare.gov/pubs/f_homstu.cfm, accessed on 7 November 2014.

Cicchetti, D. (2013) 'Annual research review: Resilient functioning in maltreated children – past, present and future perspectives.' *Journal of Consulting and Clinical Psychology 54,* 4, 402–422.

Consortium SAFE (2011) *SAFE Home study. Structured analysis family evaluation.* Available at www.safehomestudy.org, accessed on 7 November 2014.

Cousins, J. (2010) *Pushing the Boundaries of Assessment.* London: BAAF.

Crea, T., Barth, R. and Chintapalli, L. (2007) 'Home study methods for evaluating prospective resource families: History, current challenges and promising approaches.' *Child Welfare 86,* 2, 141–159.

Crea, T., Barth, R., Chintapalli, L. and Buchanan, R. (2009a) 'Structured home study evaluations: Perceived benefits of SAFE versus conventional home studies.' *Adoption Quarterly 12*, 2, 78–99.

Crea, T., Barth, R., Chintapalli, L. and Buchanan, R. (2009b) 'The implementation and expansion of SAFE: Frontline responses and the transfer of technology to practice.' *Children and Youth Services Review 31*, 903–910.

Crea, T., Barth, R., Chintapalli, L. and Buchanan, R. (2011) 'The intersection of home study assessments and child specific recruitment: The performance of home studies in practice.' *Children and Youth Services Review 33*, 28–33.

Dance, C., Ouwejan, D., Beecham, J. and Farmer, E. (2010) *Linking and Matching: A Survey of Adoption Agency Practice in England and Wales.* London: BAAF.

Department for Education (2006) *Preparing and Assessing Prospective Adopters.* London: DfE. Available at http://webarchive.nationalarchives.gov.uk/20130401151715/ https://www.education.gov.uk/publications/eOrderingDownload/00193-2006BKL-EN.pdf, accessed on 7 November 2014.

Department for Education (2011) *An Action Plan for Adoption: Tackling Delay.* London: DfE.

Derogatis, L. R., Lipman, R. S. and Covi, L. (1973) 'SCL-90: an outpatient psychiatric rating scale-preliminary report.' *Psychopharmacology Bulletin 9*, 13–28.

Donaldson Institute (2004) *What's working for children: A policy study of adoption stability and termination.* Available at www.adoptioninstitute.org, accessed on 7 November 2014.

Dibben, E. (2010) *Undertaking an Adoption Assessment in England.* London: BAAF.

Dozier, M., Lindhiem, O., Lewis, E., Bick, J., Bernard, K. and Peloso, E. (2009) 'Effects of a foster parent training program on young children's attachment behaviours: preliminary evidence from a randomized clinical trial.' *Child Adolescent Social Work Journal 26*, 321–332.

Expert Working Group on Adoption (2012) *Re-designing Adoption – Report of Expert Working Group on Adoption.* Available at www.gov.uk/government/uploads/system/ uploads/attachment_data/file/180251/working_groups_report_on_redesigning_ adoption.pdf, accessed on 7 November 2014.

Farmer, E., Moyers, S. and Lipscombe, J. (2004) *Fostering Adolescents.* London: Jessica Kingsley Publishers.

Farnfield, S. (2008) 'A theoretical model for the comprehensive assessment of parenting.' *British Journal of Social Work 38*, 1076–1099.

Fonagy, P., Steele, M., Steele, H., Moran, G. S. and Higgit, A. C. (1991) 'The capacity for understanding mental states: The reflective self in parent and child and its significance for security of attachment.' *Infant Mental Health Journal 13*, 200–217.

Fonagy, P., Steele, M., Steele, H., Leigh, T. *et al.* (1995) 'Attachment the Reflective Self and Borderline States: The Predictive Specificity of the Adult Attachment Interview and Pathological Emotional Development.' In S. Goldberg, R. Muir and J. Kerr (eds) *Attachment Theory: Social Developmental and Clinical Perspectives.* Hillsdale, NY: Analytic Press.

Fonagy, P., Target, M., Steele, H. and Steele, M. (1998) *Reflective Functioning Manual for Application to Adult Attachment Interviews.* London: University College London.

Geen, R., Malm, K. and Katz, J. (2004) 'A study to inform the recruitment and retention of general applicant adoptive parents.' *Adoption Quarterly 7*, 4, 1–28.

Gray, D. (2007) *Nurturing Adoptions: Creating Resilience After Neglect and Trauma.* Indianapolis, IN: Perspectives Press.

Green, J., Leadbitter, K., Kay, C and Sharma, K. 'Autistic Spectrum Disorder in UK adopted children.' European Child and Adolescent Psychiatry.

Groenhuijsen, L. (2009) *Handreiking Special Needs – voorlopige versie* [practice guide special needs adopter assessment – draft version]. Utrecht: Raad van de Kinderbescherming/ Child Protection Board.

Harding, R. (2012) *Barriers to adoption report.* PACT Research available at: www. pactcharity.org/docs/Barriers%20to%20Adoption%20Exec%20summary%20 Oct%2012.pdf, accessed on 7 November 2014.

Hobfoll, S. E. (1988) 'Conservation of resources: A new attempt at conceptualizing stress.' *American Psychologist 44*, 513–524.

Hoksbergen, R., Rijk, K., Dijkum, C. V. and Laak, J. T. (2004) 'Adoption of Romanian children in the Netherlands: Behavior problems and parenting burden of upbringing for adoptive parents.' *Developmental and Behavioral Pediatrics 25*, 3, 175–180.

Jones, D. (2009) 'Assessment of Parenting.' In J. Howarth (ed.) *The Child's World: The Comprehensive Guide to Assessing Children in Need.* 2nd edition. London: Jessica Kingsley Publishers.

Juffer, F., Bakermans-Kranenburg, M. and van Ijzendoorn, M. (eds) (2008) *Promoting Positive Parenting: An Attachment Based Intervention.* New York: Taylor and Francis.

Kaniuk, J., Steele, M. and Hodges, J. (2004) 'Report on a longitudinal research project, exploring the development of attachments between older, hard-to-place children and their adopters over the first two years of placement.' *Adoption and Fostering 28*, 2, 61–67.

Kidd, T., Hamer, M. and Steptoe, A. (2011) 'Examining the association between adult attachment style and cortisol responses to acute stress.' *Psychoneuroendocrinology 36*, 6, 771–779.

Lange, A. (1983) *InteractioneleProbleemOplossingsVragenlijst, IPOV* [Interactional Problem Solving Questionnaire, IPSQ]. Deventer, the Netherlands: Van LoghumSlaterus.

Leve, L., Harold, G., Chamberlain, P., Landsverk, J. *et al.* (2012) 'Practitioner Review: Children in foster care-vulnerabilities and evidence-based interventions that promote resilience processes.' *Journal of Child Psychology and Psychiatry 53*, 1197–1211.

Lipscombe, J., Moyers, S. and Farmer, E., (2004) 'What changes in parenting approaches occur over the course of adolescent foster care placements.' *Child and Family Social Work 9*, 243–255.

Lowe, N., Murch, M., Borkowski, M., Weaver, A., Beckford, V. and Thomas, C. (1999) *Supporting Adoption: Reframing the Approach.* London: BAAF.

Luteirjn, F., Starren, J. and VanDijk, H. (2000) *HandleidingNederlandsePersoonlijkheids-Vragenlijst (herzieneuitgave)* [Manual for the Dutch Personality Questionnaire: revised edition]. Lisse: Swets&Zeitlinger.

Mainemer, H., Gilman, L. and Ames, E. (1998) 'Parenting stress in families adopting children from Romanian orphanages.' *Journal of Family Issues 19*, 2, 164–180.

Matheny, K., Aycock, D., Curlette, W. and Junker, G. (2003) 'The coping resources inventory for stress: A measure of perceived resourcefulness.' *Journal of Clinical Psychology 59*, 12, 1261–1277.

Matheny, K. B., Curlette, W. L., Aycock, D. W., Pugh, J. L. and Taylor, H. F. (1987) *The Coping Resources Inventory for Stress.* Atlanta, GA: Health Prisms.

McRoy, R. G. (1999) *Special Needs Adoptions: Practice Issues.* New York: Garland Publishing.

Meins, E., Fernyhough, C., Wainwright, R., Gupta, M. D. and Tuckey, M. (2002) 'Maternal mind-mindedness and attachment security as predictors of theory of mind understanding.' *Child Development 73*, 1715–1726.

Meins, E. (2013) 'Sensitive attunement to infant's internal states: operationalising the construct of mind-mindedness.' *Attachment and Human Development 15*, 5–6, 524–44.

Mesman, J. and Emmen, R. (2013) 'Mary Ainsworth's legacy: A systematic review of observational instruments measuring parental sensitivity.' *Attachment and Human Development 15*, 5–6, 485–506.

Moon, J. A. (2004) *A Handbook of Reflective and Experiential Learning Theory and Practice.* London: Routledge.

Munro, E. (2011) *The Munro Review of Child Protection: Final Report.* Cmd 8062. London: Department for Education.

Noordegraaf, N., van Nijnatten, C. and Elbers, E. (2009a) 'How social workers start to assess the suitability of prospective adoptive parents.' *Research on Language and Social Interaction 42*, 3, 276–298.

Noordegraaf, M., Ninjnattan, C. and Elbers, E. (2009b) 'Assessing parents for adoptive parenthood: Institutional reformulations of biographical notes.' *Children and Youth Services Review 31*, 89–96

Oppenheim, D. and Koren-Karie, N. (2013) 'The insightfulness assessment: Measuring the internal processes underlying maternal sensitivity.' *Attachment and Human Development 15*, 5–6, 545–561.

O'Sullivan, T. (2004) 'Inputs to an Adoption Panel: A case study.' *Adoption and Fostering 28*, 41–51.

Quinton, D. (2012) *Rethinking Matching in Adoptions from Care.* London: BAAF.

Reder, P., Duncan, S. and Gray, M. (1993) *Beyond Blame: Child Abuse Tragedies Revisited.* London: Routledge.

Reder, P., Duncan, S. and Lucey, C. (2003) *Studies in the Assessment of Parenting.* London: Routledge.

Reilly, T. and Platz, L. (2003) 'Characteristics and challenges of families who adopt children with special needs: An empirical study.' *Children and Youth Services Review 25*, 781–803.

Rijk, C. H., Hoksbergen, R. A., Laak, J. J., Dijkum, C. V. and Robbroeckx, L. H. M. (2006) 'Parents who adopt deprived children have a difficult task.' *Adoption Quarterly 9*, 2–3, 37–61.

Rispens, J., Goudena, P. P. and Groenendaal J. H. A. (eds) (1994) *Preventie van psychosocialeproblemenbijkinderen en jeugdigen* [Prevention of psychosocial problems in children and youngsters]. Houten: Bohn, Stafleu and Van Loghum.

Rushton, A. (2003) *Adoption of looked after children a scoping review of research.* London SCIE available at www.scie.org.uk/publications/knowledgereviews/kr02.pdf, accessed on 7 November 2014.

Sar, B. K. (2000) 'Preparation for adoptive parenthood with a special needs child.' *Adoption Quarterly 3*, 4, 63–80.

Saunders, H. and Selwyn, J. (2011) *Adopting Large Sibling Groups.* London: BAAF.

Schofield, G. and Beek, M. (2006) *Attachment Handbook for Foster Care and Adoption.* London: BAAF, and see www.uea.ac.uk/providingasecurebase/uses-of-the-model/ the-assessment-of-prospective-foster-carers-and-adopters, accessed on 7 November 2014.

Schreurs, P. J. G., Tellegen, B. and van de Willige, G. (1984) 'Stress en coping: de ontwikkeling van de Utrechtse Coping Lijst.' *Gedrag:tijdschriftvoorpsychologie 12,* 101–117.

Selwyn, J. (1994) 'Spies, Informers and double agents: Adoption assessments and role ambiguity.' *Adoption and Fostering 18,* 4, 43–47.

Selwyn, J., Sturgess, W., Quinton, D. and Baxter, C. (2006) *Costs and Outcomes of Non Infant adoptions.* London: BAAF.

Selwyn, J., Wijedasa, D. and Meakings, S. (2014) *Beyond the Adoption Order: Challenges, Interventions and Disruption.* London: DfE. Available at www.bristol.ac.uk/hadley, accessed 7 November 2014.

Sinclair, I., Gibbs, I. and Wilson, K. (2004) *Foster Carers: Why They Stay and Why They Leave.* London: Jessica Kingsley Publishers.

Slade, A. (2005) 'Parental reflective functioning: An introduction.' *Attachment and Human Development 7,* 3, 269–281.

Smulders, L. and Van Tuyll, L. A. C. (2003/2004) *Assessment Guide Home Study.* Utrecht Raadvoor de Kinderbescherming (Child Protection Board). Internal publication.

Social Services Inspectorate (1993) *Planning for Permanence? Adoption Services in Three Northern Local Authorities.* London: HMSO.

Steele, M., Kaniuk, J., Hodges, J., Haworth, C. and Huss, C. (2000) 'The Use of the Adult Attachment Interview: Implications for Adoption and Foster Care.' In BAAF *Assessment Preparation and Support: Implications from Research.* London: BAAF.

Steele, M., Hodges, J., Kaniuk, J., Hillman, S., & Henderson, K. (2003). 'Attachment representations and adoption: Associations between maternal states of mind and emotion narratives in previously maltreated children.' *Journal of Child Psychotherapy 29,* 187–205.

Stroobants, T., Vanderfaille, J. and Put, J. (2011) *Evaluatie van de huidige screening van adoptieoudersuitgevoerd door Dienstenvoormaatschappelijkonderzoek van de CAW's in het kader vande geschiktheidprocedurevoorinterlandelijkeadoptiegevoerdvoor de jeugdrechtbank.* [Evaluation of the current screening of prospective adopters]. Leuven: SWVG. Available at www.kindengezin.be/img/evaluatie-screening-adoptieouders.pdf, accessed on 7 November 2014.

Turney, D., Platt, D., Selwyn, J. and Farmer, E. (2012) *Improving Child and Family Assessments.* London: Jessica Kingsley Publishers.

Ungar, M., Ghazinour, M. and Richter J. (2013) 'Annual Research Review: What is resilience within the social ecology of human development?' *Journal of Child Psychology and Psychiatry 54,* 4, 348–366.

Van IJzendoorn, M. H. (1995) 'Adult attachment representations, parental responsiveness and infant attachment.' *Psychological Bulletin 117,* 387–403.

Vinke. A. (1999) *Geschiktvoor het adoptiefouderschap? De ontwikkeling en het gebruik van eentaxatie – instrument voorgezinsfunctioneren met het oog op interlandelijkeadoptie.* [Suitable for adoptive parenting? The development and use of an assessment instrument for family functioning in intercountry adoptions]. Doctoral dissertation, Utrecht University. Delft: Eburon.

Vinke A. (2008) *Intercountry, non relative adoption in the Netherlands. Dutch report as part of an inter-European study on inter-country adoptions,* commissioned by the EU parliament. Bilthoven/Brussels/Firenze.

Vinke, A. (2013) 'Decisions in intercountry adoptions – the home study.' Presentation of a framework for assessment of prospective adopters. Workshop at the International Conference on Adoption Research, Bilbao, July.

Vinke, A. and Van Tuyll, L. A. C. (1996) *AdoptieLijstBijzondereGeschiktheid. Instructiesvoor de Raadvoor de Kinderbeschermingt.b.v. experimenteelgebruik* [Adoption Questionnaire Special Suitability – experimental questionnaire]. OudZuilen/De Bilt.

Vinke, A. J. G. and Van Tuyll, L. A. C. (1996) *AdoptieLijstBijzondereGeschiktheid. Instructiesvoor de Raadvoor de Kinderbeschermingt.b.v. experimenteelgebruik* [Adoption Questionnaire Special Suitability – experimental questionnaire]. OudZuilen/De Bilt.

Wheaton, B. (1983) 'Stress, personal coping resources, and psychiatric symptoms: An investigation of interactive models.' *Journal of Health and Social Behavior 24,* 208–229.

Wilson J., Kahn, H. and Geen, R. (2005) *Listening to parents overcoming barriers to the adoption of children from foster care.* Available at https://cbexpress.acf.hhs.gov/index. cfm?event=website.viewArticles&issueid=156&articleid=4169, accessed on 7 November 2014.

Zeanah, C., Berlin, L. and Boris, N. (2011) 'Practitioner Review: Clinical applications of attachment theory and research for infants and young children.' *Journal of Consulting and Clinical Psychology 52,* 8, 819–833.

# CHAPTER 4

# A Case Study in Assessment

## Adoptionplus

*Joanne Alper*

Adoptionplus is a therapeutic voluntary adoption agency first registered in 2008. It is based near Milton Keynes in Buckinghamshire. As the agency was being set up, and with the encouragement and support of the agency's two directors, Deborah Ferguson and Paul Snell, I spent a considerable amount of time as service director thinking about how we undertake our assessments. One of the key tasks of the agency was to find families for older children who had experienced considerable trauma. The plan was to provide these families with access to therapeutic support whenever they needed it, until their child reached the age of 18.

We knew that parenting children who had suffered abuse and neglect required a certain combination of skills and qualities in adopters, but working out how we were going to recognise and promote these skills in prospective parents was going to be a challenge. What information would be key in identifying people who would be able to manage the often high levels of stress involved in parenting children who had experienced trauma? I knew that we wanted empathetic, reflective and fun people who would be able to manage their own emotional experiences and be able to deal with the emotional impact of parenting children who would bring their own unresolved trauma into the family home. These potential parents would need to be able to think about things from the child's perspective, manage their own stress, ask for help when needed and have realistic expectations of themselves and of their child.

We therefore needed an assessment process that could help us to identify which people had these qualities, or the potential to develop them. As social workers I'm sure we have all worked with people who we thought would be good adopters or foster carers, yet when a child was placed, the competent, coping image that they gave us crumbled leaving a very different person standing there. During the assessment, people may have said that when faced with challenging parenting situations, they would respond in a certain way. For example, saying that they would not take rejecting behaviour personally, and that they would consider the reasons underlying their child's behaviours. They would speak of understanding that these difficult behaviours were likely to be linked to early abusive parenting, and needed to be responded to with understanding and compassion. Additionally, many of these parents would say that they would be comfortable asking for support should difficulties arise.

However, once the child was placed and appearing to reject them, these parents would often respond very differently. I'm sure many of us have known parents who have resisted support and become angry and punitive towards the child. Some parents even reject the child leading to placement disruption. The emotional responses they were experiencing when they were feeling rejected turned out to be completely different to the cognitive view they had had of themselves prior to the placement. In these cases, not only would the social worker be surprised by their response, but also in many cases, the adopters themselves would be surprised and unprepared by their own feelings and response.

When designing our new assessment process, I wanted it not only to help us understand and appreciate prospective parents, but also to help them better understand and appreciate themselves. I believed that it was important that both the assessing social worker and the parent, through the assessment process, developed a greater understanding of their hopes, dreams, fears and, most importantly, how they might behave when under stress. We needed people to feel safe enough to be honest with us and to think about and understand themselves as openly as possible. As part of this I was aware that it was important to identify what the key qualities and factors were in successfully parenting a child who had experienced trauma, and clarify how an assessment process could help identify who had those qualities.

## Lighting the way

Setting up a new agency was actually quite liberating in many ways. Yes, it required lots of form filling and procedure writing, but it also gave me the opportunity to stop and really think about what we wanted to do and how we wanted to do it. We didn't have to undertake assessments in a certain way just because that's the way they were always done. I could design a new assessment process that I believed could help us gain a more realistic idea of parenting capacity, particularly parenting capacity under stress. No assessment process of potential parenting capacity would be foolproof but I wanted to make it as effective as possible.

During this period I found the writings of Dr Dan Siegel and Dr Dan Hughes really helpful and thought provoking. Dan Hughes' PACE model helped direct me to the value of Playfulness, Acceptance, Curiosity and Empathy. It seemed to me such a kind approach to parenting, one that promoted both greater understanding and the development of delicate, new parent-child relationships. When thinking about the pain, confusion and fear that must surround, and at times engulf children who have been abused and neglected by the very people who should have been the ones to protect them, a PACE approach just felt right.

Dan Siegel and Mary Hartzell's book, *Parenting from the Inside Out* (2014) took me further on the journey of understanding compassionate parenting: compassion both for the child and the parent. These ideas guided me as I began to develop ways of assessing parenting capacity that focused more on analysis and understanding.

Selwyn *et al.* (2011) believe that analysis and reflection are essential in social work assessments, and that intuition must also be allowed to play its part.

> Effective thinking in social work – making use of an assessment mindset – involved the careful use of a range of different 'thinking approaches'. We have identified that practitioners need to be able to draw on both analytical and intuitive modes of thought. In addition, these need to be accompanied by an ability to think both critically and reflectively. (Selwyn *et al.* 2011, p.87)

I would argue that an over emphasis on checklists and a devaluing of the relationship between the assessing social worker and the prospective parent can limit the quality, depth and potential usefulness of assessments. Not only is the relationship the key vessel of a parenting assessment but also an understanding of our own humanity enables us to connect with people on a much deeper level.

When training as a social worker in the 1980s I was encouraged to be objective when making decisions, consider the research and ensure I didn't allow my personal feelings to bias my judgement of a situation. Thirty years on I believe these factors remain important. However, as a human being as well as a professional, I have increasingly come to value the role of my own feelings in situations. I believe they should be listened to and considered as they are part of our social skill set and tell us something about ourselves, our experiences and/or the people we are communicating with.

Learning about Steven Porges's description of the Vagal system was so validating, reassuring me that our 'gut feelings' are in fact connected to our brain. Dr Jonathan Baylin explains more about this in Chapter 7. The contribution of intuition and 'gut' feeling to any assessment, although potentially valuable, should still be considered with caution. Effective supervision is always critical to help recognise and counter the risks of personal bias. The key issue for social workers in these situations is to consider what our 'gut' feelings are about and where they belong. Is it a personal issue that belongs to us or is it something that belongs to the prospective adoptive or foster parent? These feelings are like little flags that our bodies are waving, saying 'notice me'. You could almost argue that they are gifts your body gives you during an assessment, advising you to check something out or explore something in more detail. Clearly personal bias has no place in assessment. However, that shouldn't mean that intuition and gut feeling should be discounted.

## The maps that matter

Dan Siegel stated in a presentation he gave at Woburn Abbey (Adoptionplus, Woburn Abbey 2013) that in relationships we need to have in our minds:

- a me map
- a you map
- a we map.

I find this really helpful, a beautifully simplified way of explaining the complexities of what is really important. Adoption is clearly all about relationships: the child's relationship with their adoptive parents and the adopters' relationship with the social workers assessing, preparing and supporting them. We are trying to identify people who are aware of their own thoughts and feelings, can understand the thoughts and feelings of other people, and recognise how the two impact each on the other. Essentially we are looking for people who are good at relationships – making them, maintaining them and repairing them.

## Embracing the 'we map'

In order to assess a prospective parent's capacity for this level of reflection, I was clear that we would require a staff team with similar skills to those we were looking for in our prospective parents. We needed our social workers to be sensitive, warm people who were aware of their own feelings and could tune in to the needs and feelings of others. I thought that these attuned, warm and insightful social workers were likely to be better at building relationships with prospective adopters. In my experience it was through the relationship that prospective adopters would feel safe enough to explore their feelings and better understand themselves just as in the same way the child feels safe enough in their relationships with their adoptive parents to explore their feelings and to understand themselves and their history.

I believed that we needed to recruit social workers who could model an approach and style of communication and relationship building that I considered key to achieving successful adoptions. People often talk of a 'trickle down approach' when describing a model for shared learning. I was seeing it more as a rock pool approach. Social workers and prospective parents would explore the rock pools together, being curious together, embracing both the delight and the unexpected. By being curious about, recognising and accepting our own humanity, strengths and fragilities, we could help others understand and accept their own humanity, strengths and fragilities as well as those of their adopted child. By modelling this approach, I hoped that adopters would remain curious about themselves and their child. This approach to assessment is based on understanding as opposed to judging. This approach seeks to encourage a real understanding of people and how they might parent without making them feel defensive.

The agency itself has a vital role to play in developing and maintaining this approach. We couldn't expect attuned, warm and sensitive social workers to remain that way if we, as an agency, didn't also take care of them. I wanted our social workers to feel valued, appreciated, accepted and not criticised. As an agency we had to accept that people would make mistakes. As human beings we all make mistakes. It's not helpful for social workers, parents or adopted children to feel scared or ashamed about making mistakes. It was essential to work in a way that accepted our shared humanity whilst at the same time retaining a commitment to learning from the mistakes we did make. Ultimately we want children to understand from their parents that they are only human and they will occasionally get things wrong. We want the children to know that their parents recognise how hard they are trying, even if they do make mistakes. So, even when mistakes are made, we want children to know that they are still cared about and valued. It is clear that it is unhelpful for adopted children to be pushed into feeling shame as it just promotes a destructive sense of self and negative patterns of behaviour.

So if we wanted to encourage parents to respond in this way to their children, then we need to respond in this way to their parents. Furthermore, the agency also needed to respond in this way to its staff if we were to remain true to this approach. I think this way of working makes sense as it promotes a commitment to effective practice, where time and energy is spent improving, as opposed to spending time defending or covering things up.

## What are the key qualities and how do you know if people have them?

Rushton (2004) in his scoping review of adoption research, states that various factors have been proposed as positive indicators in successful placements: 'child centeredness, warmth, consistency, flexibility, tenacity, a sense of humour, a capacity to reflect on problems and their origins' (Rushton 2004, p.91). However there is no clear research evidence linking these with outcomes. He suggests that outcomes are likely to depend on an interaction between factors in the child, the parent and the context.

In thinking about the qualities we are looking for when undertaking assessments, it is important to be aware that the presence of certain key parenting qualities is only part of the contribution to the success of an adoptive or foster placement. Without the support families need, these qualities on their own may not be enough. Support is crucial and can be central to the successful parenting of some adopted and fostered children. Beesley (2010) agrees stating that 'on-going support...is essential' (p.176). The research study *Beyond the Adoption Order* (Selwyn, Wijedasa and Meakings 2014) highlights some extreme challenges faced by adoptive families. Additionally, the government's increasing recognition of the importance of effective adoption support can be seen in the investments it is currently making in this sector. Thus, in thinking about the qualities we are looking for in prospective parents, an important aspect involves looking for qualities that assist parents in being able to access and accept support.

Adoptionplus's longstanding therapeutic support services have given us the opportunity to work with a large number of families in their care of their fostered and adopted children. It appeared that people who possessed many of the key parenting skills we were looking for were also the ones who found it easier to access the support that was offered, understand the more complex underlying causes of some of the difficulties, and implement the advice suggested regarding their parenting approach. Importantly, they were also more likely to be open to considering the part they might be playing in contributing to the difficulties and how best they might respond to bring about a solution.

In addition, we also believe many of the characteristics and qualities we are looking for are not necessarily fixed but can change and develop over time. Dance and Rushton's study (2005) of children placed in middle childhood found that maternal sensitivity increased over time for some mothers, suggesting that this is not necessarily a fixed characteristic, but is one that can develop and increase with the right support. When thinking about the qualities and characteristics we would ideally like to see when undertaking assessments we have become increasingly convinced that we are also looking for the potential for growth and development. Beesley (2010) writes 'Parenting capacity develops alongside parenting the child. The challenge for the assessing social worker, in many cases is being able to predict parenting capacity in relation to a hypothetical child or children' (Beesley 2010, p.175).

As part of the assessment journey of increased understanding, I also gained considerable insight from travelling around the country providing training on Parent Assessment Reports (PARs)/ Form F assessments to hundreds of local authority adoption and fostering social workers. This training was provided to the many local authorities keen to enable their social workers to improve the quality of their PAR assessments. This was in response to the BAAF introduction of an updated PAR which included new sections on analysis and encouraged reports to be more concise, and new assessment guidelines requiring social workers to complete PARs in a much shorter time frame. The contributions to this book of the many experienced and skilled social workers I spoke to during the course of that training cannot be overstated. It is one thing for a professional like me to develop my own views and perspectives based on my own and my team's experiences and research. It is quite another to hear the views of hundreds of other professionals working in the same field. Their insight, knowledge and experience further helped solidify my views about the qualities needed to successfully parent children who have experienced developmental trauma. So what are the qualities that social workers have highlighted as important?

- empathy, warmth, nurturing, and the ability to continue to offer these even when the child appears to reject them

- flexibility and the capacity to manage loss, change, pain and grief

- the ability to ask for help and support

- openness, and a willingness to learn and be cooperative

- the ability to be accepting of difference and our own human frailties: realistic expectations of themselves and their child

- being playful and the ability to have fun and enjoy spending time with children

- being good at relationship building, maintaining and repairing relationships, and resolving conflict

- good reflective functioning and potential for mind-mindedness

- no unresolved past trauma issues

- ability to regulate when stressed.

The next step in the assessment journey was to consider how to gather this information and in particular, how to gather this information within increasingly tight timescales.

## Understanding the how: What tools could be helpful?

We might know what the areas are about which we should like to gather information, but the issue is how do we actually gather this information?

When considering this in the development of Adoptionplus assessments, I thought it would be useful to explore whether there were assessment tools already in existence that could help to shine a light on some of these complex areas.

As part of this exploration I undertook training in both the Attachment Style Interview (ASI; Professor Bifulco) and reflective functioning training on the Parent Development Interview (PDI) (Fonagy *et al.* 1998).

Both tools offer something to the development of a deeper level of understanding of the prospective parent. The ASI has assisted us in gathering helpful information about a person's support networks. We found the reflective functioning training particularly helpful. The term reflective functioning refers to the ability to think about thinking and think about feelings, both our own thoughts and feelings and the thoughts and feelings of others and the impact we have on others' thoughts and feelings and the impact of theirs on us (Fonagy and Target 1997).

Although the reflective functioning training on the PDI coding system is usually used as a research tool, as social workers we found it helpful in assisting us with our parenting assessments. This tool felt like a gift as it eloquently helped steer us to look at and think differently about all the information we received. It felt like I was putting on a pair of glasses; the image before me may have been the same, but the way I viewed it was very different.

Recently we have also been exploring the use of the 'Self-Compassion Scale – Short Form' (SCS-SF) (Raes *et al.* 2011). The scale is the shortened version of the Self-Compassion Scale (Neff 2003). Measuring self-compassion can give an indication of kindness to the self, which may contribute to better understanding how a person may be able to take care of themselves when stressed. In Chapter 5, Kim S. Golding and Ben Gurney-Smith explore this in more detail and consider research into the links between stress, mind-mindedness and compassion.

However, none of the tools we use gives us all the information we need. They need to be used with caution and with the understanding that it's not only what qualities people can evidence now that are important, but also the potential they have for growth and development. The assessment is a journey and is actually a tool in itself that can be used as part of the assessment. Social workers need to ask the question 'In what way has this person changed since the assessment began?' At Adoptionplus we aim to ensure that the same social worker works with the prospective adopter through stage one and stage two, giving them a longer period of time to develop a relationship and really get to know the individual applicant. Clearly, this also allows the social worker to see how the person changes and develops during the process, as they learn about the children who have suffered developmental trauma and the parenting they require.

At Adoptionplus, none of these assessment tools is used to rule people in or out. We just use them as part of the overall assessment as we aim to achieve a better understanding of the prospective parent.

## Understanding the how:
## The social work task

In the past, some social workers might have been tempted to identify whether a person has the qualities we are looking for by just asking them. For example:

> Social worker: 'Are you good at making relationships?'

> Prospective parent: 'Yes very good. My friends are important to me. I'm always there for them when they need me.'

> Social worker: 'That's great. Thanks. Now on to the next question…'

This limited type of interaction fails to explore the response, makes no attempt to test the response and will severely restrict the scope for a rigorous analysis. When thinking about an alternative approach to collecting this information, it is helpful to consider what information would be needed to really understand whether a person is good at maintaining relationships. The social worker would want to know in what ways the prospective parent thought that they were good at making relationships.

- Could they give examples of close longstanding relationships?

- What factors did they believe were important in making and maintaining relationships?

- Could they give examples of any disagreements they had had with close friends or family?

- How were they resolved?

- Who approached who first?

- What was said?

- How did they feel about the other person's response?

- How did they think the other person felt about their response?

- Were there similar patterns in relationship resolution?

- Did referee visits back up what the prospective parent had said?

This deeper level of questioning and exploration provides a more comprehensive understanding of the parent's ability to make, maintain and repair relationships. At the same time as these questions are explored we would also want to consider evidence of mind-mindedness and reflective functioning. In their responses about disagreements, for example:

- Did the prospective parent have an understanding of how the other person may have felt?

- Were they able to think about how their actions/thoughts/ feelings may have affected the other person, or how the other person's thoughts/feelings or actions could have affected them?

- Could you see them actually thinking and processing the information as they were sharing it with you?

- Were they congruent in their emotional affect when they discussed painful or upsetting issues?

All of these things and many more can provide the social worker with a wealth of information. Considering the increasing restrictions of assessment time, it really is important for us to make the most of all the information with which we are being provided.

So how else can we, as social workers, use the resources available to us to assess whether an individual has the qualities required to parent a child who has experienced developmental trauma?

# Suggestions and ideas that could promote understanding

Box 4.1 lists a number of suggestions that could help promote increased understanding of a person's prospective parenting skills, strengths and weaknesses.

---

**BOX 4.1 SUGGESTIONS AND IDEAS THAT COULD PROMOTE BETTER UNDERSTANDING OF PARENTING CAPACITY**

**Empathy, warmth and nurturing**
As one human being to another, I believe it is important when considering this question to consider how they are in their relationship with you. How are they when you meet them? Do they show sensitivity or awareness of your comfort? Listen to your 'gut feeling', your vagal nerve is telling you something. However it's important to check out if it is telling you something about them or yourself. It's also important to consider how the prospective adopter's referees describe them. Does it fit with your experience of them? Have you observed them with other people? If they have undertaken voluntary work with children, what feedback have you had from that organisation?

**Flexibility and not having rigid or fixed expectations of self and others**
Can they give examples of when they have had to adapt and be flexible at difficult times in their lives? How flexible are they during the assessment if the situation has needed to change? Are they open to changing their views on things when they receive new information? Are they open to hearing other people's perspectives? Have they changed their view on something during the assessment and preparation training having learnt more about it?

---

**Open and willing to learn**

Are they interested in and curious about the information they receive during assessment and preparation training? Do they ask lots of questions indicating a desire to develop a deeper understanding? Do they read the books and articles suggested? Do they have further comments and questions in relation to them? Are they able to say if they don't understand something or if they find something difficult? Are they open to thinking about and talking about their childhood and difficult experiences? Are they open to considering new ideas?

**Good at relationship building maintaining and repair**

Children who have experienced abuse and neglect by their birth parents are likely to find building trusting relationships really difficult and challenging. Being able to build and maintain healthy relationships is central to emotional and psychical well-being and, as such, this is an area in which their adoptive or foster parents need to have strong skills.

When assessing a prospective parent, social workers could consider and explore whether they have longstanding close friendships. You could ask them to talk about relationship difficulties. How were they repaired? Who starts the repair? How is it resolved? Can they understand the situation from the other person's perspective? Do they show any empathy for the other person's feelings? Were they able to approach the other person when needed to initiate the repair? Can they take responsibility when they make a mistake? Can they apologise? You could ask about a relationship difficulty they may have had with their partner or a referee. You could then check with the other person about their perception of the repair.

**Reflective functioning and potential for mind-mindedness**

- Can you see the prospective parent thinking in the room and reviewing something they had previously thought or felt?

- Do they present as curious and interested in why others might feel or behave the way they do?

- Do they acknowledge and tolerate not always knowing what others are thinking and feeling, while at the same time trying to understand?

- Can they accurately attribute the mental states of themselves and others?

- Can they envision the possibility that feelings concerning a situation may be unrelated to the observable aspects of it?

- Do they have recognition of diverse perspectives?

- Can they take into account their own mental state in interpreting other people's behaviour?

- Can they take an intergenerational perspective, making links across generations?

- Can they revise thoughts and feelings about childhood in light of understanding gained since childhood?

- Do they show any evidence of emotional attunement?

**Being able to manage their own stress and pressure – knowing what 'pushes their buttons', what the signs are when they are starting to feel stressed, and what action they need to take to manage the situation**
Ask them for specific examples, exploring what they did, whether they asked for help, how others responded and how they then responded. Explore what they think may hinder them at times of stress, what they themselves may do that doesn't help. Do their partner and referees support their description of themselves? It's important that people are able to 'stay with' painful thoughts and feelings in order to explore and understand them.

If they avoid their own emotional pain they are going to find it difficult to help a traumatised child understand and make sense of their pain.

When exploring these areas, we have also found the response to distress questions in the Adult Attachment Interview (AAI) helpful to consider:

- Childhood
  - When you were distressed/upset what did you do? Describe an actual event.
  - When you were ill/or hurt yourself what happened? How were you cared for? Describe an actual event.

- Adult
  - When you are distressed or upset now what do you do? Give an example of one time when you were upset.
  - When you are feeling ill what do you do?
  - How do you take care of yourself?
  - Is there a difference when you feel a little unwell, to when you are feeling very ill?
  - Can you give examples of how you take care of yourself when you feel ill?

- Integrative
  - Do you think that your childhood experiences influence how you deal with stress now? If so, in what ways?

### Ability to ask for and accept support

When considering an individual's ability to ask for support we have found the ASI helpful as it requires people to give specific examples. At Adoptionplus our experience is that being able to ask for and accept support when needed is an essential part of successfully parenting a child who has experienced developmental trauma. During an assessment you may wish to explore specific difficulties the person has had in the past and how they were able to ask for support. If they had difficulty asking for support it would be worth asking them what they felt stopped them or got in the way.

**Resolved issues of loss and trauma/coherent narrative**

'Discourse is judged coherent when a subject appears able to access and evaluate memories while simultaneously remaining plausible and collaborative consistent, clear, relevant, and succinct' (Main, Goldwyn and Hesse 2008). A coherent narrative is a description of past events that appears believable and true to the listener. As a social worker you will be considering: Are the person's feelings about the events they are talking about consistent with the events they are describing? For example, do they laugh when discussing someone dying?

- Are they able to put across the information clearly without contradiction?

- Can the person work collaboratively with the social worker to clarify what information is required, and then make sure that their response is understood?

- As the social worker, can you see the person thinking and reflecting on what is being discussed?

- A key indication of incoherence would be if the person were lost in the material they were sharing and had difficulty following what was said.

- Another aspect of coherence is that the person does not provide more information than is necessary to make their point (very long answers to questions with lots of irrelevant material can suggest incoherence).

## More than assessment

In developing a philosophy and approach to making good assessments, I saw the assessment process itself as an important tool to help ensure that we knew our families well, and to help us understand the best way to support them if they became stressed or found themselves struggling.

Additionally, and most importantly, I saw this assessment process not only as an opportunity for us to learn about our prospective adopters, but for them to learn about themselves. Adopting a child who has experienced loss and developmental trauma was going to put them on a path that would take them to places that they had never been before. Thinking you know how something will feel is very different to how it actually feels. The emotional rollercoaster would be like nothing they had ever experienced. We really wanted the assessment process to help them to understand themselves better, to be able to predict the situations that would be most stressful to them and to think about why these situations had this power to cause upset and distress. We wanted the assessments to help prospective adopters understand how they themselves responded when they were stressed and what they needed to help them cope during these difficult times. We wanted to explore with them how they might spot the signs that they were beginning to struggle before things became too overwhelming. In short we wanted them to be as prepared as possible.

Knowledge and self-understanding have the potential to provide the forearming that can forewarn parents as they find themselves in different circumstances. This type of assessment process not only helps us to identify parents who could adopt successfully, but can also be a tool in helping parents manage the ups and downs of the adoption journey. Importantly, it is also a process that begins the support relationship between the parents and the adoption agency. How we manage the assessment process influences how easily the adopting parents can recognise their need for support and how willing they are likely to be in seeking such support from us.

The assessment process is therefore a journey of discovery together, side by side, learning about each other, and what is likely to be needed to help make the placement a success. We want to be curious with them, and help nurture that curiosity like a tender little seedling, feeding it, protecting it and helping it grow so that its strong roots take hold enabling the adoptive parent to stay curious and present. We want the parents to stay curious about themselves and why they feel the way they feel or respond the way they do. We want them to remain curious about their child and why he or she responds the way they do. We see the assessment process as the foundation of this open and curious approach.

As social workers we have a relatively small amount of time to assess people and help them prepare to become adoptive parents. At the outset, one of the things I wanted the assessment process to achieve was to make sure we used the time we had as effectively as possible. I realised that we could model the approach with them that we wanted them to use when parenting. I wanted staff at Adoptionplus to model an approach that was curious, respectful, sensitive and open. Although it is clear that we are assessing them as potential parents, we didn't want them to feel judged. That's quite a tricky thing to achieve. We knew that people have to feel reasonably safe if they are going to be open with us about their feelings. It is clear that the skill of the assessing social worker is of central importance. The social worker has to impart certain key messages: (1) I'm genuinely interested in getting to know you; (2) I'm not going to make assumptions about why you feel the way you feel or why you respond the way you do; (3) I'm not expecting you to be perfect; (4) and we are all human and we all make mistakes. As well as helping prospective parents to feel comfortable enough to be open with the social worker we also hope that these same key messages will be ones that adoptive and foster parents can impart to their children.

## Conclusion

Adoption and fostering are all about people and relationships. In order to assess whether an individual has the capacity to adopt or foster a child who has experienced trauma, you have to really understand them. To understand them, they really need to feel safe and comfortable with you as the assessing social worker. We believe that the best and most effective way to do this is through developing and strengthening a trusting relationship between the social worker and the prospective parent. Alongside this we believe that there are a number of assessment tools that can helpfully contribute to this process. We have been particularly interested in tools that help us better understand both a person's reflective functioning and ability to manage stress.

When designing an effective assessment process at Adoptionplus, I was repeatedly drawn towards a model that promoted compassionate parenting, one in which there was compassion for both the child and the parents. I also believed that the assessment process itself had the potential to provide so much more than just a PAR or Form F to assist in decisions regarding approval and matching. It could help the parent on their own journey of self-discovery, it could identify adoption support needs and, importantly, it could promote the development of a trusting relationship between the parents and the agency. This in turn could encourage parents to contact the agency when difficulties arise without fear of criticism or blame. After all, in the scheme of things, although important, the assessment is really only a very small part of the adoption or fostering journey. Families have their whole lives ahead of them. Using this pivotal process to help prepare and support them on this journey seems a sensible way forward. Ultimately the assessment process is not an exact science. Thinking about how you may parent is quite different from the realities of parenting, and the assessment process can only go so far. There will always be people who surprise us and themselves with their actual response to parenting. Although we can try to undertake as thorough an assessment as possible, there will still be times when things are missed. The value in the assessment process is therefore not solely its conclusion, but the relationships built, messages given and understanding gained along the way.

# References

Beesley, P. (2010) *Making Good Assessments*. London: BAAF.

Dance, C. and Rushton, A. (2005) 'Predictors of outcome for unrelated adoptive placements made during middle childhood.' *Child and Family Social Work 10*, 4, 269–280.

Fonagy, P. and Target, M. (1997) 'Attachment and reflective function: Their role in self-organization.' *Development and Psychopathology 9*, 679–700.

Fonagy, P., Target, M., Steele, H. and Steele, M. (1998) *Reflective Functioning Manual, Version 5, For Application to Adult Attachment Interview*. London: University College London.

Main, M., Goldwyn, R. and Hesse, E. (2008) *The Adult Attachment Interview: Scoring and Classification System*. Berkeley, CA: University of California.

Neff, K. D. (2003) 'The development and validisation of a scale to measure self-compassion.' *Self and Identity 2*, 223–250.

Raes, F., Pommier, E., Neff, K. D. and Van Gucht, D. (2011) 'Construction and factorial validation of a short form of the Self-Compassion Scale.' *Clinical Psychology and Psychotherapy 18*, 3, 250–255.

Rushton, A. (2004) 'A scoping and scanning review of the research on the adoption of children placed from public care.' *Clinical Child Psychology and Psychiatry 9*, 1, 89–106.

Turney, D. Platt, D. Selwyn, J., and Farmer E. (2011) *Improving Child and Family Assessments: Turning Research into Practice.* London: Jessica Kingsley Publishers.

Selwyn, J., Wijedasa, D. and Meakings, S. (2014) *Beyond the Adoption Order: Challenges, Interventions and Adoption Disruption.* London: Department for Education.

Siegel, D. and Hartzell, M. (2014) *Parenting from the Inside Out.* London: Scribe Publications.

CHAPTER 5

# Parenting Well and Staying Well

## Understanding the Qualities Needed for Parenting Children with Developmental Trauma

*Kim S. Golding and Ben Gurney-Smith*

Imagine your worst fear; perhaps spiders or maybe snakes. You may have a specific fear linked to an experience that you had earlier in your life. Think about what happens in your body when you encounter reminders of this fear. It might be a photograph, a movement in the corner of the room or perhaps something more tangible, coming face to face with the feared object. You will notice your heart rate increasing as your body goes on high alert. You might clench your fists ready to attack or perhaps your whole body feels restless as you are preparing to run. Deep in your brain your amygdala is sounding the alarm and your body is preparing for fight or flight. Your focus narrows as you try to manage your fear; you cannot focus your attention on anything else; you barely hear what others are saying to you. The fear becomes all-encompassing.

Now imagine that your worst fear is not a spider or a snake, an object that you will only meet occasionally. Imagine instead your fear is of being parented: being hurt by a parent or worse still being neglected, denigrated or abandoned by the people who are meant to keep you safe. What will trigger this fear for you? What will remind you of this fear? It is not being with strangers. You will feel relatively safe with people who are not trying to care for you. With this experience in your past it will be intimate relationships that trigger your alarm system. Others wanting to take care of you, nurture you, discipline you; in other words being parented becomes the most likely trigger for putting your body into a state of alarm.

Imagine what it is like as a child living day to day with your worst fear being activated. Now imagine you wake up, day after day, in a relationship with your child that is unpredictable, stressful and often painful. The day-to-day experience of living in a relationship with someone who demonstrates quick changes in emotional states and who refuses your comfort and kindness is exhausting and troubling. As a consequence, your original hopes and dreams of the parent you thought you could be begin to fade and seem distant and almost naïve. There are few moments of joy. At times your child looks at you as if you mean harm, even when you have been gentle and understanding. You begin to think you are the cause of the problems. You notice it becomes easier to withdraw from the relationship rather than to try to get close and be hurt again. To compound your sense that you are failing the relationship, your child seems closer with other people. You feel bound by obligation and yet you begin to question yourself like never before. Your efforts to comfort your child are resisted and you doubt your own ability to be effective. You find it difficult to read your child's needs, you fear getting too close and you question your original commitment to being this child's parent. You become self-critical, defensive, reactive, short-tempered and stressed.

In these scenarios both parent and child are in a fundamental dilemma that can profoundly affect the success and health of their relationship. This dilemma marks out a unique feature of altruistic parenting relationships seen in adoption and fostering. Whilst the foster or adoptive parents set out to be the children's greatest source of comfort and safety, the children view their parenting as the greatest source of danger and insecurity. This dilemma usually has its origins in the children's earliest attachment experiences. In response to their earliest needs for safety and security, they have had little or no comfort, kindness has been withdrawn or they have experienced frightening and harmful adult behaviour. The impact on the children can fundamentally affect their development and their capacity to enter into reciprocal and secure relationships. These features are characteristic of 'developmental trauma' (see Chapter 2).

Aside from the commitment, resources and support important for any parent, adoptive and foster parents need a particular resilience to help the children feel safe being parented and, while doing so, to remain healthy and well. In thinking about the unique qualities that foster and adoptive parents need it is important to keep the dilemma of parenting children who are frightened of being parented central to any assessment of future capacity. In this chapter we focus on the qualities that foster parents and adopters need if they are to successfully parent children who have found the experience of being parented previously so traumatic. We consider how assessments of prospective adoptive or foster parents might be informed by this understanding.

## The relevance of stress when parenting children with developmental trauma

Synthesizing the research that underpins our understanding of the caregiving brain, Hughes and Baylin (2012) outline how stress can affect or 'block' parenting capacity. Our focus in this chapter rests on what they term 'child specific blocked care'; that is, the potential for the child's insecure attachment behaviours, due to developmental trauma, to be the source of stress. In this way, the term parenting stress refers to psychological distress linked to parenting a child. This may involve the perception of the child as difficult (Abidin 1995). We outline the research, where available, from adoption and fostering studies, noting where there are indicators helpful to assessing prospective adoptive or foster parents.

Whilst foster and adoptive parents are likely to be affected by the same things that stress other parents, such as poor social support, recent research has shown that parenting can be more challenging and stressful for them. A recent UK study found higher rates of parenting stress for adoptive parents compared with parents of biologically related children (Harris-Waller 2012; Harris-Waller Granger and Gurney-Smith submitted). Interestingly, studies of foster carers using the same measures do not show higher rates of overall parenting stress (e.g. Granger 2008) but do indicate that the perceived difficulties of the child lead to higher rates of stress than for biological parents (e.g. Gabler 2013).What therefore makes adoptive and foster parents more likely to experience parenting stress?

Harris-Waller (2012) explored how some of the difficulties that often characterize the children placed for adoption impact on parenting stress and compared this to the experience of biological parents. For both adoptive and biological parents, parenting stress went up when attachment difficulties and behaviour problems in the child were more severe. However, as anticipated, the rates of difficulties in the child were much higher for adoptive parents and this made them much more vulnerable to higher stress levels. Studies of foster carers seem to show a different picture. For example, where foster carers have been studied who show strain, a similar concept to stress, this is associated with the perception of difficulties in the child rather than the levels of difficulties *per se* (Farmer, Lipscombe and Moyers 2005). The implications from these findings are that the risk of increased stress in fostering and adoption may be higher than for biological parents but there may be different mechanisms depending on whether the parenting is via fostering or adoption. Either way resilience to stress will be an important quality to consider in both prospective foster and adoptive parents.

How might living with a child with attachment difficulties affect the adoptive or foster parent? Foster carers who report strain caring for adolescents were found to be less likely to be engaged with their foster children and were less effective at parenting with limits (Farmer *et al.* 2005). Granger (2008) also found that lower levels of stress lead to greater ratings of secure behaviour towards their foster children.

By measuring a concept called 'mind-mindedness', studies have shown how stress may affect not just the behaviour in the relationship but also the thinking about the child. Mind-mindedness is defined as the 'proclivity to treat the child as having a mind' (Meins 1997). More specifically, it is the proportion of time in which the parent describes the child's mental states, rather than maintaining a narrow focus on outward behaviour or physical appearance, that typifies more mind-minded relationships. For example 'thoughtful' is a mind-minded description rather than 'active' or 'attractive', which emphasize behaviour and appearance and not the mental life of the child. Mind-mindedness is seen as a positive quality and has been associated with lower parenting stress (McMahon and Meins 2012). An increased ability to be mind-minded predicts positive behaviour in the child (Meins *et al.* 2013). Whether the parent uses positive, negative or neutral words to describe the child's mind is also important (Demers *et al.* 2010). This is referred to as 'valence'; for example, a positive mind-minded description would be 'clever', a neutral one 'he likes', and a negative mind-minded comment would be 'stupid'. Positive mind-mindedness has been associated with lower levels of parenting stress in biological parents (Demers *et al.* 2010; McMahon and Meins 2012).

A recent study comparing adoptive parents with biological parents found that the mind-mindedness of parents does seem to be affected by stress, attachment difficulties and the behaviour of the child (Harris-Waller 2012; Harris-Waller *et al.* submitted). They found that for both adoptive and biological parents, the greater the difficulties they reported, the greater their stress and the more likely it was they would describe their child's mind in negative ways. The study also found that even despite the level of difficulties being higher in adoption, adoptive parents have a tendency to be more negatively mind-minded than their biological counterparts. Further research is needed to explain this difference. It is suggested that studies looking at mind-mindedness over a longer time period may help answer such questions. However, when it comes to adoption, it does point to the impact on the type of thinking parenting children with higher levels of attachment difficulties and problematic behaviour can have. In foster care, the valence of mind-mindedness and parenting stress has not been studied, but Granger (2008) conducted an earlier, exploratory study of parenting stress in foster care and found that some aspects of mind-mindedness worsened in foster carers if they reported greater parenting stress. Taken together, these findings point to the importance of understanding how stress can deeply affect a parent including the way their think about their child's mind and just how vulnerable adoptive parents are likely to be in this way. Understanding potential ways to address stress in adoptive parents is therefore an important area for further study.

Building on these findings, Glossop (2013) investigated whether parenting stress in adoption could be linked to attributes shown to be associated with mental well-being such as mindfulness and compassion (Brown and Ryan 2003) and might offer ways of preparing adoptive parents for stress or helping them treat it successfully. For the purposes of this chapter, it may help to understand how mindfulness and compassion are relevant to the qualities associated with resilient parenting, and are therefore useful abilities to consider in the assessment process.

Mindfulness describes one's ability to deliberately focus attention on feelings, thoughts and experiences in the present moment and in a non-judgemental and accepting way (Kabat-Zinn 1990). Compassion is described by Gilbert (2005) as 'being open to the suffering of self and others in a non-defensive and non-judgmental way' (p.1). Training in mindfulness has been developed as an evidence-based intervention for a number of conditions including depression and those living with chronic pain (e.g. Kabat-Zinn 1990). It has been found to significantly reduce parenting stress and can increase the use of social support, improve the relationship with the child and reduce the child's behaviour difficulties (see Harnett and Dawe 2012).

Given the high rates of parenting stress found in adoptive parents, Glossop (2013) investigated, for the first time in an adoptive sample, mindfulness, self-compassion and parenting stress alongside the attachment difficulties of their children. As predicted, they found that adoptive parents' levels of mindfulness and compassion towards themselves went down as parenting stress went up. Despite the strong relationship between stress, compassion and mindfulness, the extent of the perceived attachment difficulties of the child was found to be even more predictive of stress than how mindful or compassionate the parent was. This finding points to the importance of considering the extent of the impact of the child's attachment difficulties on parenting stress alongside the prospective parent's capacity to be mindful and compassionate (Glossop, Granger and Gurney-Smith submitted).

One of the scenarios that opened this chapter described the painful feelings which can arise for parents when their child rejects or withdraws from care and comfort. The studies in this section, when taken together, illustrate how important attachment difficulties are when it comes to understanding higher rates of parenting stress in adoption and fostering. More specifically it is the difficulties in the relationship and not just the level of emotional and behavioural difficulties in the child that are important. Prospective parents and foster carers will need available support and intervention to help them address the difficulties their children bring if they are to remain healthy and well. The research also suggests that they need to be open to help not just for their children but also for themselves: in other words to show compassion to themselves *and* their children.

Studies are yet to be conducted looking at the effectiveness of mindfulness and compassion training in adoption and fostering, but the evidence presented here suggests they are worthy of investigation. A quality of openness to help and the capacity to see how their own needs may impact on their relationship with their child, both in behaviour and in mind, are likely to be important when assessing for resilience in prospective parents. It may also predict whether they can accept help for their own difficulties and those in their child. Prospective parents will need to be open to the possibility that whilst they might be changed to the good by their children, this may also be in ways that they did not predict, expect or want. More research is needed if we are to understand this unique parenting experience more fully and comprehend how children may 'block' the parenting they need to recover from early trauma.

Understanding the stressful nature of parenting developmentally traumatized children is therefore an important consideration when assessing prospective adoptive and foster parents (see Box 5.1). Resilience to stress will be an important factor in their successful parenting. The qualities needed to parent developmentally traumatized children are considered in the next section alongside pointers for the assessment of these qualities in line with the sections of the prospective adopter's report (PAR) (BAAF 2013) referring to parenting capacity.

**BOX 5.1 POINTS TO CONSIDER WHEN THINKING ABOUT PARENTING STRESS IN ADOPTIVE AND FOSTER PARENTS**

- Attachment, emotional and behaviour difficulties are more likely in adopted and fostered children and make parenting stress a vulnerability for parents of these children.

- Parenting stress is highly relevant to fostering and adoption although the mechanisms of what causes this stress may differ – more research is needed.

- How stress is managed in relationships now may be an important area to consider when predicting how well prospective parents may manage stressful relationships with their children in the future.

- Parenting stress for adoptive parents and foster parents is associated with a negative change in behaviour and thinking towards the child.

- Mindfulness and compassion might buffer the risk of parenting stress for prospective adoptive and foster parents, but more research is needed.

- Self-compassion *and* compassion for others may be important when understanding parenting stress, resilience and openness to help.

- Adoptive and foster parents who can see how their behaviour can be changed by their relationship with their child are likely to be open to help for themselves and not just their child.

# Qualities needed for parenting developmentally traumatized children

Figure 5.1 provides a model for thinking about the qualities that foster parents and adopters need to successfully parent traumatized children (Golding 2014). This involves qualities that can be used to help children feel safe, and develop relationships alongside the daily task of managing what can be highly challenging behaviour. We will consider that the capacity to be mind-minded and its relationship to parenting stress and the ability to demonstrate PACE (playfulness, acceptance, curiosity and empathy) as a compassionate parenting attitude are core to providing this parenting (see Hughes 2009; Golding and Hughes 2012). With these qualities in place, parents are more likely to be able to provide healing parenting that helps children discover safety in being parented and to have reciprocal and rewarding relationships. The children will discover the secure base of family life, and the comfort of dependence gained from this will help them develop autonomy and a healthy independence. Security will allow growth and exploration of the world. The children will develop a capacity to enter and sustain relationships. They will be able to manage boundaries on their behaviour because of the connection that these relationships bring.

In this section we will use the model pictured in Figure 5.1 to explore the qualities parents need when parenting developmentally traumatized children. This requires:

1. A resilient sense of self: Resilience will be based on a good knowledge of self and capacity to reflect on others. This is central for holding onto an attitude of PACE and connecting with the child through mind-minded parenting.

2. Ability to offer a secure base: Enhanced parenting skills are needed to provide therapeutic parenting that allows the children to discover security in being parented. This will be based upon an understanding of the child's development of attachment behaviours. The child has learnt a way of being in the world that allows him to feel safe without a secure base. The parent now needs to help him learn to give up these patterns of relating so that he can use the parent as a secure base.

3. Ability to build relationships: Enhanced parenting skills also develop the child's capacity for relationships. This rests on the ability to provide authoritative parenting that offers an unconditional relationship alongside warmth and clear boundaries matched to the child's developing autonomy.

4. Ability to manage behaviour: Alongside therapeutic parenting, enhanced behavioural management skills are needed that provide containment for behaviour whilst maintaining an emotional connection with the child.

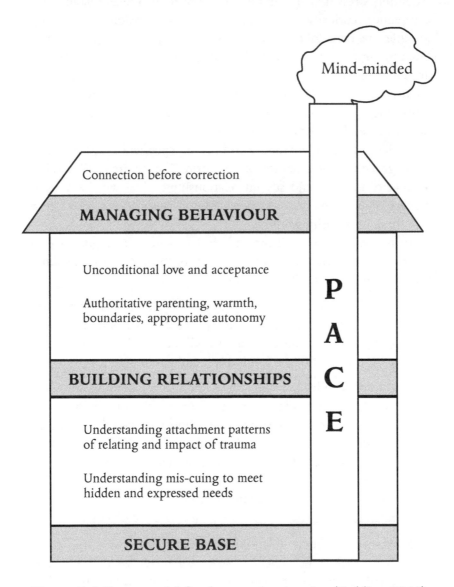

**Figure 5.1** House model for therapeutic parenting (Golding 2014)

For each part of the model, we will outline both what qualities prospective adoptive parents may need and what to look for in assessment. When making recommendations for assessment of the parenting qualities we have identified, we duly recognize that social work assessments are being made in a vacuum of research using longitudinal studies. These studies are needed if we are to be more confident in predicting the qualities that are critical to successful parenting, impacting positively on future family lives. The following points are based on what we understand about parenting stress in adoptive and foster parents and the theoretical concepts known to be critical to resilient parenting. Our suggestions are made with due respect to the tension between needing the best informed approach now and the absence of an evidence base.

## Resilience based on a good knowledge of self and capacity to reflect on other (see Boxes 5.2 and 5.3)

A resilient parent is likely to be one who has high reflective functioning (Fonagy *et al.* 2002; Allen 2013). At its core this rests on a capacity to think about thinking; to be metacognitve (Main 1991). More specifically, it is the ability to recognize that one's thoughts and feelings can have an effect on the other's thoughts and feelings. We use our cognition when we think. When we know and can reflect on our thinking we are demonstrating metacognition. A dog thinks about food: 'Are you going to feed me?' and will not play with the toy being offered. A human notices himself thinking about food and how this is distracting him from the activity he is trying to do ('I am feeling hungry, I won't succeed with this until I have had something to eat').

Noticing oneself thinking rests on the ability to mentalize: to understand the mind and the internal experience of thoughts, feelings, beliefs, joys, worries, doubts and fears of this mind. Humans are self aware, able to notice what they or others are thinking and feeling, to step outside of immediate experience and reflect on its impact.

Imagine a parent trying to get a child ready for bed whilst the child is determined to continue playing. The parent starts to get angry. The parent with good reflective functioning will:

Notice herself getting angry and recognize the child is having this impact on her.

Be aware of deeper fears; resting on thoughts and feelings that 'getting angry' symbolizes. 'I am feeling like a useless parent. I think that I will never parent successfully.'

Know that this is a fear she holds which may or may not be true, but is perhaps related to earlier attachment experience.

Understand the self, and therefore can now focus on the child and see how her behaviour may be affecting her child's ability to go to bed. She will be able to wonder why the child does not want to go to bed. For example, this child always gets anxious at bedtime, she worries that a man will climb through the window and take her.

Understand the child, which leads to successful support for the child; for example, demonstrating that the window is locked; reading a story, which helps the child feel safe; using a baby monitor so that the child can hear her moving around downstairs. As a result the parent will accomplish the parenting task of putting the child to bed.

The ability to use one aspect of reflective functioning can be seen in parenting that is mind-minded (Meins 1997). The parent who is psychologically attuned to the child is able to make inferences about the child's internal experience that she can use to emotionally connect with the child. For example, the parent might say to the child: 'It seems like you really don't want to go to bed; I wonder if that is why you are running away from me. I am wondering if going to bed is scary and you might be worried that someone might come through the window and take you. I know it is hard, I would like you to see how safe the house is and how safe I can help you feel. No one can get in and I will be close by to make sure you are safe all night.'

Mind-minded parenting is an important part of being able to maintain the parenting attitude of PACE. This attitude is recommended for parenting children with developmental trauma and a high level of attachment insecurity (Hughes 2009). The attitude of PACE relies on qualities of Playful parenting, Acceptance of the child's inner world, Curiosity about the meaning underneath the behaviour and Empathy for the child's emotional state. This enables the child to feel accepted, understood and emotionally attuned with the parent (Golding and Hughes 2012). Parents who are able to feel curious even at the most stressful moments for them and their child, who can accept and empathize with the child's emotional discomfort even when they are emotionally discomforted, and who can be appropriately playful based on a genuine enjoyment of their relationship with the child will find PACE comes fairly naturally.

Reflective functioning, leading to mind-minded parenting and the ability to use an attitude of PACE, and to return to this when it is lost under stress, is central to the qualities of parenting that provide security, build relationships and manage behaviour.

---

**BOX 5.2 QUALITIES NEEDED FOR A RESILIENT SENSE OF SELF**

- Good reflective functioning, which may be seen in a capacity for mind-mindedness within relationships.

- Capacity for curiosity even at stressful times.

- Acceptance of emotional discomfort and distress.

- Able to show empathy for child's internal experience.

- Able to enjoy the relationship and be playful at appropriate times.

**BOX 5.3 DOES THE PROSPECTIVE PARENT HAVE THE QUALITIES NEEDED FOR A RESILIENT SENSE OF SELF?**

Look for:

- Examples of reflective functioning; for example, ask about the impact of past and current relationships; explore attachment and other relationship experiences. Can the parents understand the impact of significant life events upon themselves?

- Notice what happens to reflective functioning when stress increases. Does the parent stay reflective or become more reactive and defensive?

- Can they be *positively* mind-minded and use PACE when with children, for example, experience in their nursery placement, with nieces and nephews or children of friends?

- Ask the potential parent to relate simple incidents with others – notice mentalizing language (referring to the mind of the child), capacity to be curious, empathic and accepting. Can they talk for the other person's experience of them?

- Does she have a sense of fun in relationships or is humour used to convey criticism or used in a less connected way?

## Secure base: Enhanced parenting skills that provide therapeutic parenting based upon an understanding of the child's development of attachment behaviours (see Boxes 5.4 and 5.5)

Children who have been highly insecure or frightened within their early experience of being parented will adapt to this level of fear through the attachment patterns that they adopt. These represent a way of relating to parents and other potential attachment figures that reduces the sense of danger and increases a sense of safety (Crittenden *et al.* 2001). Developmentally traumatized children will display highly controlling patterns of relating that are coercive, self-reliant and resist connection with parents (Golding 2008). The children feel safer avoiding attuned connection with the parent, taking control of the relationship instead. This, however, has a detrimental impact on their development, ability to explore and learn in the world, and ultimately to have successful friendships and relationships.

Successful parenting of these children will rest on a good understanding of the different attachment patterns and the implications of these in the way that children miscue the parent (Dozier 2003). Being able to 'read' the child is an important aspect of what Hughes and Baylin (2012) call 'mindful parenting'. This is often challenged when parenting children who do not signal their needs clearly due to attachment difficulties. Developmentally traumatized children will signal their need, not based on their internal sense of comfort or discomfort, but based on their expectations of the parent. Thus a pattern of hidden and expressed needs is displayed.

For example if the child expects that the parents will withdraw when they perceive that he needs comfort he will hide the need for comfort, expressing instead a need for exploration (avoidant attachment pattern). The developmentally traumatized child will display controlling patterns of self reliant, compliant and/or caregiving behaviours in order to hide emotional neediness.

On the other hand, if the child expects that the parents will be inconsistently available and unpredictable in their responses to the child he will hide a need for exploration and express a need for comfort instead (ambivalent resistant pattern). The developmentally traumatized child will display controlling patterns of highly coercive, attention-needing behaviours in order to hide comfort with exploration.

Sensitive parenting is important to raise healthy children, but to parent children with these insecure and controlling patterns of relating the sensitive parent has to also be gently challenging (Dozier 2003). In other words parents have to be attuned and sensitive to both the expressed and the hidden needs through an understanding of the miscuing the children display. They need to provide parenting that helps the children to feel safe and secure and over time reduces the children's need to miscue. This comes from a capacity to be compassionate to both the children and themselves and to maintain a belief that they can be the source of comfort for their children even when the children behave in a way that may reject this. At worst this can lead to the parents questioning their own motivations in their relationship with their children.

---

**BOX 5.4 QUALITIES NEEDED TO OFFER A SECURE BASE**

- Understanding attachment patterns and ability to recognize a child's miscues.
- Sensitive parenting that can also be gently challenging.
- Rests on ability to emotionally attune to child.
- Good support.
- A capacity to be mindful.
- A compassionate stance to themselves and their child.

---

**BOX 5.5 DOES THE PROSPECTIVE PARENT HAVE THE QUALITIES TO OFFER A SECURE BASE?**

- Ask about difficult and challenging relationships; consider attachment relationships specifically, as this will elicit the key elements of reflective capacity when under stress.
- Are they able to recognize the emotional experience of the other and attune to this? Is the parent sensitive to the signals from others; able to attune to the needs being signalled and thus accept and cooperate with what the other needs? Does the parent want to understand what another needs or does he or she tend to tell people what they need?

---

- Can the parent understand that needs can be expressed and hidden? Do they have sufficient flexibility to be both sensitive and gently challenging?

- Do they have good supportive relationships? Do they recognize they may have hidden and expressed needs when it comes to their behaviour in relationships? Ask them to reflect on how they express their needs and if appropriate how they hide their hidden needs? Notice if they tend to downplay their needs and for what reason.

- Look for and ask for examples of sensitivity and insensitivity in relationships. Would they confide in this person? Do they feel listened to?

- Consider how the parent manages stress particularly when they have felt responsible or bad about their behaviour or actions at the time. Do they show compassion to themselves *and* any other person involved? Do they now look back and forgive themselves for any mistakes or behaviour they regret when stressed or are they closed to their own contribution? Do they seek help when stressed and when do they seek help?

## Build relationships: Enhanced parenting skills that develop the child's capacity for relationships (see Boxes 5.6 and 5.7)

Research carried out in the 1970s identified the parenting style that was most likely to be associated with confident children able to successfully develop autonomy (Baumrind 1978). Baumrind called this *authoritative* parenting, describing this as parenting that is high in warmth, provides clear and consistent boundaries, and provides the child with an appropriate level of autonomy. This is not to be confused with *authoritarian* parenting, which is more punitive, and reduces a child's development of autonomy.

The capacity to offer authoritative parenting will be associated with healthy relationships between parents and children. It is therefore important for foster carers and adopters to be able to offer this type of parenting if they are to help children to experience and benefit from relationships. Warmth, boundaries and autonomy are related to the child's developmental age. Thus the parent needs to offer these parenting experiences tailored to the child's needs. This is complicated in developmentally traumatized children, who are often emotionally immature with an exaggerated regression to an even younger emotional age when under stress. Attachment difficulties and problematic behaviours mean that these children are likely to require more from the relationship with the parent. This is likely to put a strain on the relationship between parent and child. The authoritative parent of the developmentally traumatized child needs to be able to rapidly adjust their parenting to day-by-day changes in what the child needs in the way of boundaries and autonomy. Parents will need the capacity to be flexible as well as consistent within their parenting.

When parenting developmentally traumatized children, authoritative parenting has to additionally be enhanced to allow healing of the injuries done by the experience of traumatic relationships. The biggest injuries for children hurt within early relationships are upon their capacity to feel safe within relationships and from this secure base to enter intersubjectively into relationships. Safety develops from the experience of an attachment relationship (Bowlby 1998). Intersubjectivity develops from the experience of a contingent and responsive relationship (Trevarthen 2001). The way children come to see themselves – their sense of self – is an outcome of these intersubjective relationships. When a child's early experience of relationship involves misattunement and fear the child gains a sense of self as deficient and bad. The child learns to avoid intersubjective relationships, preferring control rather than connection with the other. Parents need to be highly resilient when parenting controlling children. The sense of failure and hopelessness that can develop when children resist connection can lead to parents withdrawing from intersubjectivity as well (as described by

Hughes and Baylin 2012). Both end up trying to control rather than connect. An important quality of parenting is therefore the resilience to continue to connect to the child intersubjectively. This allows the child over time to reduce his need for control. He can benefit from the positive sense of self that can develop when he allows himself to connect to a warm and attuned parent. This is likely to require the parents to remain open and engaged despite their own stress response (Hughes and Baylin 2012).

This in turn rests on the capacity to offer unconditional acceptance of the child's internal experience however uncomfortable or stressful that is. The child fears not being good enough. He anticipates that others will be frightening and he expects loss and abandonment. As the child experiences his deepest fears and expectations being accepted and understood he can at last begin to give them up.

Finally, helping children develop relationships also needs to provide experience of the recoverability of these relationships at points of rupture. Due to the greater likelihood of behavioural difficulties and insecure attachment behaviour in developmentally traumatized children, things will go wrong. Children need guidance from their parent about their behaviour in order to address it and learn from their mistakes. They also need parents who can convey that they can still be loved and accepted unconditionally despite these difficulties. This capacity for interactive repair, to get back to feeling connected, is likely to be vital for the child's recovery from their difficulties and their hard-held negative views of themselves.

Fortunately parents do not need to be superhuman; they will make mistakes, misattune and misunderstand the children they are caring for. Even in secure relationships, this is a common feature. The critical aspect is the capacity to recognize this through reflective and mindful parenting. An important quality for foster and adoptive parents is likely to be a capacity to take a compassionate stance to themselves if they are to be able to acknowledge their mistakes and to make repairs with their children.

## BOX 5.6 QUALITIES NEEDED TO BUILD RELATIONSHIPS

- Ability to parent authoritatively through provision of warmth, boundaries and developmentally appropriate autonomy.

- Flexibility to respond to fluctuating emotional maturities.

- A capacity to be compassionate to themselves.

- A capacity to offer intersubjective connection to children who are controlling.

- A capacity to connect with emotional distress and discomfort and offer unconditional acceptance of this internal experience.

- Ability to take responsibility for repairing relationship however the rupture occurs.

## BOX 5.7 DOES THE PROSPECTIVE PARENT HAVE THE QUALITIES NEEDED TO BE ABLE TO BUILD RELATIONSHIPS?

- Ask about their own experience of being parented and what they would like to take and reject from this experience. What do they feel that children need? Do they recognize the need for warmth and boundaries? Are they comfortable in fostering both dependence and independence or are they more comfortable with one or the other?

- Look for examples of flexibility and ability to adapt in changing circumstances.

- What intimate relationships have they experienced? Are they comfortable with reciprocity, that is, being cared for by someone they are caring for? How do they manage when relationships run into difficulties? Are they able to take the lead in repairing relationships? Do they demonstrate compassion for themselves *and* the other person or people involved?

## Manage behaviour: Enhanced behavioural management skills that provide containment for behaviour whilst maintaining an emotional connection with the child (see Boxes 5.8 and 5.9)

Traditional parenting advice has a central focus on how to manage the behaviour of the child. This rests on the behavioural principles which suggest that behaviour becomes acceptable when we consistently use appropriate rewards, sanctions and consequences. The use of such disciplinary parenting techniques does not need to begin until the end of the child's first year and beginning of his second. As the child becomes mobile, the world opens up to him, and limits on his behaviour keep him safe (correction). Without the need for this discipline in the early months the parent can instead focus on providing the child with an experience of unconditional love and acceptance (connection). This is essential for the child to develop trust in the parent, and to develop his sense of self as someone who is loveable and trustworthy. Without this first experience the child develops mistrust and a sense of his own badness (Erikson 1959). Foster carers and adopters don't often have the opportunity to parent the child in their formative first years of becoming socialized. They therefore enter into the parenting of the child once mistrust has been established. They need to provide parenting that rebuilds trust alongside providing limits on behaviour. Instead of correction building on top of a well-established connection, the parent needs to do the connection and the correction at the same time.

In order to do this the parent needs qualities of flexibility, being able to attune to the child's internal emotional experience and connect with this whilst also being mindful of the child's external behaviour and need for boundaries around this.

Understanding and connecting with emotional experience is important but not always easy. Children can be very uncomfortable when they experience understanding and emotional connection. Children may initially hold on more strongly to their controlling behaviours, and can become angry and aggressive as they experience threats to this way of relating to others. The parent will have to manage being on the receiving end of a large amount of controlling behaviours within which the child attempts to restore the status quo. It is easy at these times to become reactive to these behaviours and thus to be pulled into confrontational interactions. Parents will need the capacity for flexible responding and a large amount of impulse control if they are to stay reflective rather than reactive at these times.

---

**BOX 5.8 QUALITIES NEEDED TO MANAGE CHALLENGING BEHAVIOUR**

- Understand and adapt parenting techniques.

- Ability to connect with child whilst providing correction of behaviour.

- Flexibility of responding.

- Good impulse control.

- Ability to attune to internal experience whilst managing external behavior.

---

**BOX 5.9 DOES THE PROSPECTIVE PARENT HAVE THE QUALITIES NEEDED TO MANAGE CHALLENGING BEHAVIOUR IN A CHILD?**

- Explore their attitude to discipline. What is its purpose to them? Ask them to consider their experiences of being disciplined as a child.

- Look for their ability to be flexible, warm and responsive in relationships when unwanted behaviour has affected them. Consider their ability to hold onto the importance of the relationship yet gently challenge the behaviour that has affected them.

- Do they recognize the need for boundaries for development?

- Explore impulsivity: have they been able to manage the impulse to react defensively and if not how did they behave? Did they repair the effects of their impulsive behaviour?

- Look for ability to connect, correct and repair within relationships.

# Conclusion

Parenting children who have been developmentally traumatized is highly stressful, not least because being parented is the primary trigger for the children's fear. As children become resistant to the parenting that is on offer the parents can find themselves doubting their ability or their capacity to continue. Self-compassion, retaining mindfulness and an openness to interventions can contribute to the maintenance of resilience in the face of this challenge. Research with adoptive and foster parents has increased our understanding of parenting stress and resilience. This can inform the assessment of prospective adoptive and foster parents, although further research is needed to understand the origins of parenting stress, the impact it can have on the parent–child relationship and what interventions might help.

The resilient parent additionally needs a range of qualities that can help the children to heal from the trauma of their pasts. At the core of resilient parenting is the ability to adopt a PACE attitude to parenting based on the capacity for mind-minded parenting. This in turn can help the parent to provide a secure base, which facilitates relationship development and helps the parent to stay connected to the child whilst also managing the range of challenging behaviours that are being displayed.

In this chapter, these qualities have been explored with recommendations for their assessment. This supports the attachment-focused approach found in the PAR (2013).This offers specific questions and areas for further exploration by skilled social workers to assist with the deeper analysis of one of most demanding and yet critical social work tasks, the assessment of prospective foster and adoptive parents.

# References

Abidin, R. R. (1995) *Parenting Stress Index* (3rd edition). Odessa, FL: PAR.

Allen, J. G. (2013) *Mentalizing in the Development and Treatment of Attachment Trauma.* London: Karnac Books Ltd.

BAAF (2013) *Prospective Adopter's Report.* London: BAAF.

Baumrind, D. (1978) 'Parental disciplinary patterns and social competence in children.' *Youth and Society 9*, 238–276.

Bowlby, J. (1998) *A Secure Base: Clinical Applications of Attachment Theory.* London: Routledge (Original work published 1988).

Brown, K. W and Ryan, R. M. (2003) 'The benefits of being present: Mindfulness and its role in psychological well-being.' *Journal of Personality and Social Psychology 84,* 4, 822–848.

Crittenden, P. M., Landini, A. and Claussen, A. H. (2001) 'A Dynamic-Maturational Approach to Treatment of Maltreated Children.' In J. N. Hughes, A. M. La Greca and J. C. Conoley (eds) *Handbook of Psychological Services for Children and Adolescents.* Oxford: Oxford University Press.

Demers, I., Bernier, A., Tarabulsy, G. M. and Provost, M. A. (2010) 'Maternal and child characteristics as antecedents of maternal mind-mindedness.' *Infant Mental Health Journal 31,* 1, 94–112.

Dozier, M. (2003) 'Attachment-based treatment for vulnerable children.' *Attachment and Human Development 5,* 3, 253–257.

Erikson, Erik H. (1959) *Identity and the Life Cycle.* New York: International Universities Press.

Farmer, E., Lipscombe, J and Moyers, S. (2005) 'Foster carer strain and its impact on parenting and placement outcomes for adolescents.' *Journal of Social Work 35,* 2, 237–253.

Fonagy, P., Gergely, G., Jurist, E. L. and Target, M. (2002) *Affect Regulation, Mentalization, and the Development of the Self.* New York: Other Press.

Gabler, S. D. (2013) 'Foster children's attachment development and mental health in the first six months of foster care placement: Associations with foster parents' stress and sensitivity.' Unpublished Dissertation, Friedrich-Alexander-Universität, Erlangen-Nürnberg.

Gilbert, P. (2005) *Compassion: Conceptualisations, Research and Use in Psychotherapy.* London: Routledge.

Glossop, A. (2013) *What is the relationship between mindfulness, self-compassion and parenting stress in adoptive parents?* Unpublished doctoral thesis, University of Oxford.

Glossop, A., Granger, C.E. and Gurney-Smith, B.J. (submitted) *What is the Relationship between Mindfulness, Self-Compassion and Parenting Stress in Adoptive Parents?*

Golding, K. S. (2008) *Nurturing Attachments: Supporting Children Who are Fostered or Adopted.* London: Jessica Kingsley Publishers.

Golding, K. S. (2014) *Nurturing Attachments Training Resource: Running Groups for Adoptive Parents and Carers of Children Who Have Experienced Early Trauma and Attachment Difficulties.* London: Jessica Kingsley Publishers.

Golding K.S. and Hughes D. A. (2012) *Creating Loving Attachments: Parenting with PACE to Nurture Confidence and Security in the Troubled Child.* London: Jessica Kingsley Publishers.

Granger, C. E. (2008) 'The role of the reflective function of foster carers in the quality of long-term foster placements: An exploratory study.' Unpublished doctoral thesis, University of Oxford.

Harnett, P. H. and Dawe, S. (2012) 'The contribution of mindfulness-based therapies for children and families and proposed conceptual integration.' *Child and Adolescent Mental Health 17,* 195–208.

Harris-Waller, J. (2012) *Parenting stress, parental mind-mindedness, and child behavioral characteristics in biological and adoptive families.* Unpublished doctoral thesis, University of Oxford.

Harris-Waller, J., Granger, C., and Gurney-Smith, B. J. (submitted) *Parenting stress, parental mind-mindedness and child behavioural characteristics in late adopted and biological families.*

Hughes, D. H. (2009) *Attachment Focused Parenting: Effective Strategies to Care for Children.* New York: W.W. Norton.

Hughes, D. A. and Baylin, J. (2012) *Brain-based Parenting: The Neuroscience of Caregiving for Healthy Attachment.* New York: W.W. Norton.

Kabat-Zinn, J. (1990) *Full Catastrophe Living: Using the Wisdom of Your Body and Mind to Face Stress, Pain and Illness.* New York: Delacourt.

McMahon, C. A. and Meins, E. (2012) 'Mind-mindedness, parenting stress, and emotional availability in mothers of preschoolers.' *Early Childhood Research Quarterly* 27, 2, 245–252.

Main, M. (1991) 'Metacognitive Knowledge, Metacognitive Monitoring, and Singular (Coherent) vs Multiple (Incoherent) Model of Attachment.' In C. M. Parkes, J. Stevenson-Hinde and P. Marris (eds) *Attachment Across the Life-cycle.* London: Routledge.

Meins, E. (1997) *Security of Attachment and the Social Development of Cognition.* Hove: Psychology Press.

Meins, E., Muñoz-Centifanti, L. C., Fernyhough, C. and Fishburn, S. (2013) 'Maternal mind-mindedness and children's behavioral difficulties: Mitigating the impact of low socioeconomic status.' *Journal of Abnormal Child Psychology 41,* 543–553.

Trevarthen, C. (2001) 'Intrinsic motives for companionship in understanding: Their origin, development, and significance for infant mental health.' *Infant Mental Health Journal 22,* 95–131.

# CHAPTER 6

# Understanding Developmental Trauma, Parental Attachments, Caregiving and PACE

*Dan Hughes*

In a most fundamental way, giving birth to a child is a promise, a promise to provide safety, care, guidance and love during the child's developmental years, if not for a lifetime. This promise permeates all aspects of the child's life, giving him a sense that the relationship that he has with his parent is permanent, 'for better or for worse'. Every perception, thought, feeling and dream that emerges within the child is influenced by this promise. And when this promise is broken, it represents a betrayal of trust like no other.

Forms of such a betrayal represent the main causes of developmental trauma disorder. Child abuse – physical, sexual, emotional and verbal – breaks the promise of 'I will take care of you' given to a child at birth. Neglect – physical, emotional and mental (not thinking of your child for long periods of time) – also violates the terms of the promise. This is the trauma of absence, possibly a greater violation than are specific acts of abuse. Abandonment – 'I have other things to do' – says to the child that the promise was not worth keeping.

Breaking this promise places the child at high risk for developmental trauma disorder, which has pervasive and long-lasting consequences (Cook, Spinazzola, Ford *et al.* 2006). There are impairments in:

- attachment
- biology
- affect regulation
- cognitive functioning
- dissociation
- behavior control
- self-concept.

When one or two adults adopt a child they are making a similar promise: 'Trust us that we (I) will take care of you.' But this promise is more difficult than the one just mentioned for both the adoptive parent and the adopted child. The adoptive parent promises to help her child to unlearn her mistrust for parents, learn to trust again, and successfully engage in the developmental tasks that were undermined as a result of the original betrayal. The adoptive parent says that she will care for her child 'for better or worse' regardless of the child's success in undoing the results of the broken promise. The adoptive parent knows that her new child's mind, heart and body have been broken, and she promises to care for the child so that he may trust again, heal and proceed with his development. The adoptive parent says, 'I know that you have been broken, and I promise to help you to become whole again, and this promise will be kept whether or not you are able to do so.'

One might think that for the adopted child the promise would be such a wonderful gift that he would not be able to refuse it. He would welcome its arrival wholeheartedly because he finally was given what he wanted intensely from the moment of conception. Frequently this is not the case. He does not trust such a promise. Being hurt the first time, hurt at the core of his being, he is often unwilling and unable to trust again. Possibly at his core he would like to trust but is not able to find a way forward.

Adoptive parents certainly are aware of the importance of their promise to their new child. They have every intention of keeping it, no matter how hard doing so proves to be. They are aware of its importance, of how damaging it will be to their child if they fail to provide him with the care that he needs in order to develop well. They also know that it will be hard to raise him well. They have been told that it will be hard by a social worker and possibly by other adoptive parents. They have read about the problems that are often evident in the children who they are likely to be able to adopt. But they have faced other hard tasks in their lives and managed them well. Maybe this will be harder still, but they know how committed they are and they are confident that they will be able and willing to do whatever it takes to make the adoption successful. Their confidence is supported by friends and family who know them and know how competent and hard-working they have been throughout their adult lives. After all, they are adults – committed, caring and competent adults. It might take a while, but certainly the child who they adopt would eventually come to know and love them for who they are.

What sometimes makes it harder than they would ever dream that it might be? What makes it hard for professionals to understand that even the best intentioned, motivated and capable adoptive parents might find the adoption promise to be too difficult for them to keep?

What adoptive parents – and we professionals – often overlook is that parenting a child who does not trust, who rejects the comfort and joy, guidance and daily care that they are offering, will require them to call upon everything that they ever learned about parenting from their own parents when they were children learning to trust. Providing care for a child who has considerable difficulty forming a secure attachment will place great stress on the adoptive parents' own attachment patterns formed years before. If the parents' patterns are not characterized by attachment security and resolution, then the continuous stress of trying to raise a mistrusting, rejecting child, makes it very possible that the parents will not be able to provide the level of ongoing care that this child requires to begin to trust and develop well.

Good caregiving involves the same regions and systems in the brain that were first developed within attachment relationships (Hughes and Baylin 2012). If a parent was securely attached during her own childhood, these systems developed in a robust and integrative fashion. Then, as an adult, when she becomes a parent, these same systems are now activated again through her caregiving behavior. If her own attachment patterns were insecure or disorganized as a child, then she is at risk of having significant weaknesses in her caregiving patterns.

Also, given that caregiving patterns involve the same regions of the brain as attachment patterns, they both function best in the presence of a reciprocal response from the other, whether it be the parent or the child. When the child's attachment patterns are active and there is a failure of an appropriate caregiving response, the attachment pattern may become insecure or disorganized. When the adult's caregiving patterns are active and there is a failure of an appropriate attachment initiative or response from the child, the parent's caregiving pattern is at risk of becoming weak or unstable. When this occurs, the parent is described as manifesting 'blocked care', where the ongoing acts of caregiving become hard to consistently perform. When the parent at risk of blocked care also has an insecure or unresolved attachment pattern herself, this risk is even greater.

Assisting a child who has a disorganized attachment pattern to become securely attached to his new parent is greatly aided by the new parent's own attachment pattern. If the new parent manifests a secure attachment herself, and if she has resolved past attachment problems in her relationships with her parents, then her adoptive child is much more likely to form a secure attachment pattern with her. This finding has been demonstrated with foster parents (Dozier *et al.* 2001) and adoptive parents (Steele *et al.* 2003). Let us briefly consider the forms of attachment patterns there are and the possible influence of the parent's pattern on her child's developing pattern.

## Attachment classifications

Within all parent–child relationships, the best predictor of the child's attachment pattern is the attachment pattern of his parent. It is easy to understand why this might be so. There are four primary attachment classifications from early childhood throughout adulthood. They are:

- *Avoidant* (child) or *Dismissive* (adult). In this pattern the child or adult tends to rely primarily on self rather than others when under stress and to emphasize a rational approach to situations rather than an emotional one.

- *Ambivalent* (child) or *Preoccupied* (adult). In this pattern the child or adult tends to rely a great deal on others rather than on self and to approach situations more emotionally than rationally.

- *Disorganized* (child) or *Unresolved* (adult). Under specific stress the individual is inconsistent in his response and often overwhelmed by the situation, being unable to rely successfully on either self or others, with insufficient rational or emotional skills to manage it.

- *Secure* (child) or *Autonomous* (adult). In this pattern the individual is often able to rely successfully on self and/or others to manage stress and shows an approach to the situation that integrates the rational and emotional.

The manner in which the parent manages stress (relying on self and/or other and approaches stress (with reason and/or emotional responsiveness) is likely to be the pattern of attachment that she evokes in her child. Also, the pattern of engagement that she prefers in any situation, whether it is emotional or rational, or an integration of both, is likely to cause a similar pattern in her child.

If an adoptive parent has not developed an autonomous attachment pattern in her own life, it is going to be very difficult for her to help her adopted child to develop such a pattern when that child has already developed a very insecure, or even disorganized one. Even if a parent does manifest an autonomous attachment pattern, she may face great challenges helping her child to develop an organized attachment pattern in general and a secure one in particular. But if her pattern is dismissive, preoccupied and/or unresolved, this challenge might prove too great for her to overcome if she is to successfully enable her adopted child to become securely attached to her.

Let's consider for a moment why this might be so. In a well-functioning parent–child relationship there evolves a synchrony between attachment and caregiving, with one in rhythm with the other. The child's attachment behaviors elicit a caregiving response, and when such a response is readily available, the attachment behaviors are expressed readily and openly by the young child as the situation calls for them. The child trusts in his parent's response to his help-seeking behavior. Meeting his needs, whether physical or psychological, is given high priority by his parent. This child trusts that he is safe regardless of changes in his daily environment, if his parent is nearby.

In such a relationship, the parent too, assumes that when her child experiences distress, he will make her aware of it and then respond positively to the attuned care that she provides. Her care is valued by her child and not rejected. If she is sensitive to his needs and responds in a timely manner, why would he reject her care? When an adopted child brings an insecure or disorganized pattern to the relationship, the child is not likely to respond in a reciprocal manner to the adoptive parent's caregiving behaviors. This lack of synchrony makes it difficult for the parent to continue to provide care in the absence of a congruent response from the child. This parent is at risk of experiencing blocked care.

This difficulty is likely to be most evident when the adoptive parent manifests an unresolved attachment pattern. When her child is manifesting intense distress, often secondary to his history of developmental trauma, the adoptive parent is likely to be at risk of reacting to her child's distress with acute dysregulation herself. His trauma history, now manifested in his highly dysregulated behavior, is likely to activate similar unresolved traumas from her own attachment history. In such situations the parent is likely to become either frightening to her child or frightened by her child's intense emotional state (Lyons-Ruth and Jacobvitz 2008). Either way, she is not able to provide her child with the emotional strength and responsiveness needed for him to begin to develop an organized and secure attachment pattern in response to stress.

Apart from such triggers, the adoptive parent who does not manifest an autonomous attachment is likely to have difficulty responding to her child's intense and unpredictable behaviors because of her own challenges that are secondary to not having had a secure attachment during her own development. She is likely to have difficulty regulating her own affective states because affective regulation is facilitated by attachment security. As a result, when she is under stress due to her child's difficult behaviors, she is likely to be at risk of reacting with intense emotional outbursts, whether of rage, terror or despair. Also, securely attached individuals tend to have much better reflective functioning than do individuals without attachment security. Reflective functioning enables one to stop, inhibit one's first reaction to challenging behaviors, and then reflect upon it, making sense of its meaning and so better understand it and become better able to design the most appropriate response.

Here are three examples of child-rearing problems secondary to the parent's own attachment insecurities or lack of resolution:

1. Nine-year-old adopted boy, John, frequently has rage outbursts in response to routine frustrations and discipline. His adoptive father, Stan, often reacts to John's rage by screaming himself, along with threats and very punitive consequences. Stan had been raised in a very strict, verbally aggressive manner by his own father. When he hears John's rage, he often re-experiences his own father's treatment of him, something that he had never been able to resolve.

2. Twelve-year-old adopted girl, Sarah, would spend long periods of time by herself in her room, showing little enjoyment of spending time with her adoptive mother, Jennifer. Often, while Sarah was in her room, Jennifer would become sullen and withdrawn, feeling rejected by Sarah as not being a good enough mother. Jennifer's own mother spent a great deal of time away from the family, and when she was at home, she seldom seemed to enjoy being engaged with Jennifer. As a child, Jennifer felt that she was not a good enough daughter. When that old experience was activated by Sarah's seemingly rejecting behavior toward her, Jennifer withdrew defensively and was not able even to begin to facilitate Sarah's desire to spend time with her and to begin to rely on her.

3. Five-year-old Robert was very oppositional to the simplest expectations that his adoptive mother, Mary, would have. As a result, bedtime, mealtimes, bath times and even play times contained many conflicts and resulting frustrations for Mary. The professional told Mary a number of times that Robert's behavior was due to his developmental trauma but in the

heat of the moment, Mary would still most often react with either anger or withdrawal. Mary was experiencing blocked care because of the repeated failure in her efforts to establish an attuned, reciprocal relationship with Robert. Providing him with care seldom led to any increase in his attachment behaviors. Mary became increasingly reactive to his behavior, with less reflective functioning and emotional regulation.

Thus, we can see that for an adoptive parent to be successful in facilitating her child's attachment pattern so that it becomes more secure, it is helpful that the parent has an attachment pattern herself that is secure (autonomous). However, at times even when the parent is autonomous herself, her child still has great difficulty forming a secure pattern. This could be the case for months or years. Such a situation places the adoption itself at great risk. For this reason, specialized parenting is often necessary in order to facilitate the development of the adopted child's attachment pattern.

## Assessing a parent's attachment history and ongoing attachment patterns

In trying to determine whether the parent has attachment patterns that will provide the parent with strengths in raising an adopted child who is presenting pervasive developmental challenges, it is crucial that the professional understands as fully as possible the parent's own attachment history. Questions about the parent's history certainly must include whether or not the parent was exposed to traumatic events such as abuse, neglect, parental death, mental illness, substance abuse, domestic violence or repeated moves and separations. Questions should also include those which ask about more routine, daily experiences that are likely to provide a clue about how the parent will manage similar situations with her adopted child. These include:

- What were the characteristics of the parent's relationships with her parents? What were the communication patterns, conflicts, joint activities and interests? Was warmth and closeness openly communicated? Were there differences in the relationships that the parent had with each of her parents?

- What was the nature of discipline? Did it seem to be harsh and inconsistent, and did each parent have a similar approach? Was physical discipline employed and was it frequent and severe? Was relationship withdrawal employed and for how long?

- When the parent, as a child, experienced distress, was she able to successfully turn to her parents for comfort and support? If not, how did her parents respond when she showed signs of distress?

- When there was a conflict, how did it end? Was the relationship actively repaired by the parent shortly after the conflict? What was the nature of the repair?

- How were emotions expressed within the family? Were members of the family able to safely express anger, sadness, fear, joy, pride, shame and love?

- What was the nature of the parent's childhood family's religious and cultural beliefs, values and practices? Are these important to the parent now? If not, what has replaced them?

During the process of this questioning the professional should often ask for specific examples of what the parent is describing. As the parent gives the examples the professional should note whether or not these memories are difficult for the parent to have and speak about. In speaking of the past does the parent become angry, sad or frightened? Are there incidents, relationships or emotions that are hard for the parent to remember and describe? How the parent is responding (emotionally and cognitively) as she remembers her experiences as a child is as important as what she remembers. Parents who remember little about their past and who also show little affect associated with the memories tend to have a dismissive attachment style. Parents who remember a great deal and who still show emotional distress associated with the memories tend to have a preoccupied attachment style. Parents who have a complete lack of memory for certain relationships or events are at risk of an unresolved attachment style. This is even more likely to be the case if the parent shows acute distress and/or mental confusion or disorientation as they try to recall past events.

On the other hand, a parent may describe very stressful past events or even traumas but is able to do so in a comprehensive, coherent manner, remain regulated while remembering and describing the events, and speak about them as if she has made sense of them and their possible impact on her life. In this case, the parent is likely to manifest an autonomous attachment style in spite of the difficult events that she faced as a child. She is likely to have resolved those events and they are not likely to present significant problems for her own parenting abilities while raising her adopted child.

## When autonomous attachment is not enough: PACE

A central feature in parenting an adopted child with difficulty forming attachment security is for the parent to maintain an attitude of engagement with her child that is characterized by playfulness, acceptance, curiosity and empathy (PACE). Such an attitude is often helpful in creating a secure attachment and hence a successful adoption, for a number of reasons.

First, the attitude of PACE often enables the parent to remain open and engaged with her child when her child is angry and defensive, thus evoking a similar attitude of being open and engaged within her child (see Chapter 8). With PACE, the parent is likely to inhibit her tendency to become defensive in response to her child's anger, thus preventing an oscillating cycle of increased defensiveness.

Second, PACE increases the parent's ability to remain regulated herself, making it difficult for the child to assert control over his parent's emotional state. Children who manifest a disorganized attachment pattern often strive to control the emotional state of their parent as a central means of trying to establish their own sense of safety. Not being able to control his parent's emotional state, the child is then more likely to move toward a relationship that is based on shared experience and communication rather than control.

Third, PACE enables the parent to respond to her child's challenging behaviors in a manner that is not reactive and predictable to the child. PACE creates an element of surprise and doubt within her child, which in turn enables the child to be more curious about and open to how his parent is engages with him. Such curiosity within the child often leads him toward being receptive to learning a new way of relating.

Fourth, PACE creates an intersubjective stance in the parent's attitude toward her child. With PACE, she is more able to remain focused on her child's experience that gives meaning to his behaviors. This enables her to respond more easily to her child's underlying meanings – often loneliness, terror, shame, despair – rather than reacting to the behavior or the surface emotion of anger. Within the attitude of PACE, the parent tends to be more aware of her child's underlying strengths and vulnerabilities, and less likely to see the behavior as simply representing her child being bad, stupid, lazy or selfish. Because of the nature of such intersubjective experiences, when the parent experiences these strengths within her child, he is also likely to begin to recognize his own strengths and develop greater reflective functioning and emotional regulation.

Fifth, PACE facilitates a sense of safety for the child when engaged with his parent. The parent is able to consistently inhibit her reactions to her child's behavior, reactions that otherwise might become harsh, punitive and threatening. With increased safety, the child is less in need of trying to achieve safety through control and more open to the parent's influence over his development.

Finally, with PACE the parent's response tends to be quite integrative of her affective and reflective communications, while at the same time eliciting similar integration in her child. Such integration is a feature of attachment security for both parent and child.

Let's now explore the unique qualities of each of the four features of PACE. Further discussion of PACE may be found in *Creating Loving Discussions* (Golding and Hughes 2012) and *Attachment-Focused Parenting* (Hughes 2009).

The parent's attitude of *Playfulness* conveys a sense of lightness and relaxed enjoyment of one another that often enables the child to begin to feel emotionally closer to his parent before he is ready for expressions of affection. Sometimes, with obvious humor and laughter, it can be a primary feature of the interaction. At other times, it is in the background, conveying a quiet enjoyment and a readiness to be comfortable with one another. It enables the child to begin to experience positive emotions when his habitual sense of shame and his expectations of negative experiences make them infrequent. Also, playfulness conveys a sense of hope that the family will get through the hard times. Playfulness expresses a core of liking the child in spite of all the conflicts.

When children have experienced trauma and loss, they often habitually experience life in a tense and vigilant manner. They may take offense easily and often think that others are 'making fun' of them. Successful efforts to increase the child's sense of playfulness are likely to have a positive impact on his ability to manage his traumatic experiences.

Playfulness facilitates spontaneous, reciprocal interactions, which are the heart of the day-to-day activities between parent and infant that facilitate attachment, as does comforting your infant when he is in distress. Playing with your child should not be a reward for good behaviors since it is a way of being together that will help the child engage in 'good behaviors'. Playfulness brings a sense of relaxed closeness between parent and child that helps both to get through the hard times.

*Acceptance*, when directed at the child's inner life of thought, feeling, wishes, plans, perceptions and memories is unconditional. This creates a strong sense of safety for the child that he – who he is at his core self – is not being evaluated. With acceptance the child gradually begins to experience that the relationship that his parents have with him is 'for better or worse'. Certainly his behaviors will be evaluated and his parents will try to influence them with directives and consequences, but such evaluations are restricted to his behavior and are not directed toward the self or the relationship. Acceptance is central in the activation of the social engagement system (see Chapter 7) as well as in attachment.

Parents sometimes believe that they should be evaluating their child's inner life. They believe that if he says that he hates his sister, thinks that his teacher is mean or wishes to drop out of school, they should try to influence him so that he changes those feelings, thoughts or wishes. When parents respond to those statements with what he 'should' feel, think or want, their child is likely to stop sharing his inner life. It is better to not judge it; be curious about it instead and have empathy for the difficult experiences that your child is sharing. By responding with PACE your child is more likely to see and consider other perspectives than if you tell him what he 'should' feel, think or want. If he is able to express to you his hatred for his sister, he is less likely to show you through actions that hurt her, and more likely to let go of his feelings of hate and become more aware of his feelings of affection for her.

*Curiosity*, as it becomes central in the parent's attitude of PACE toward her adopted child, enables her to engage with her child in a reflective manner, with the quality of mind-mindedness. Such engagements are crucial for the development of the attachment relationship and the child's own reflective functioning. Children who have experienced abuse, neglect and abandonment tend to have poorly developed reflective skills and few words for their inner life. The parent's curiosity activates the child's own sense of curiosity and helps him to begin to explore who he is in light of the differences between his life before adoption and his life now.

Curiosity is a non-judgmental stance. It is an act of deep interest and fascination with one's child. Its goal is to understand, not change, the child's inner life. Curiosity tries to have little if any assumptions about the child's behavior, but rather to approach each situation with a not-knowing stance that communicates that he is safe to explore his inner life with you. There are no assumptions that he 'should' feel, think or wish in a given manner.

As the child begins to develop his own sense of curiosity he is less likely to judge his parent poorly when she sets a limit or provides a consequence to help him with his behaviors. Abused and neglected children very often assume that their adoptive parents' motives are negative (i.e. she doesn't like me, she doesn't care what I want, I'm not important to her). As he begins to wonder about what he – and his parents – think, feel, and want, he is more likely to see things in a perspective that is influenced by safety and consistent care. With the development of his mentalization skills, he will be less likely to maintain assumptions of negative parental motives.

Finally, *Empathy* lets a parent join her child in his emotional experiences of the events of his life. This enables the child to experience the emotion along with his parent's experience of it and enables him to remain regulated, make sense of the experience and integrate or resolve it. When a child experiences such emotions alone, often he is at risk of fleeing from the emotions embedded in the experience and possibly withdrawing from it or reacting impulsively.

Empathy enables the child to experience his parent's sense of caring for him so that he can rely on his parent for comfort and support. When a child becomes able to accept his parent's empathic response to his distress, that child often begins to develop a secure attachment with that parent.

Empathy also helps your child gradually to allow himself to become vulnerable with his parent when he is in distress. He might be ready to 'go it alone' and not feel anything, or manage it with anger and defensiveness. When a parent conveys empathy – showing compassion and care in her voice and facial expressions – he may allow himself to soften, be vulnerable and accept her comfort. Empathy thus encourages the child with developmental trauma to begin to allow himself to be sad again, trusting that his vulnerability will be responded to with sufficient support to manage the distress much more effectively than efforts to manage it alone. This sequence of distress followed by comfort facilitates a developing attachment toward the adoptive parent better than any other.

## How to assess a parent's readiness and ability to maintain PACE

PACE is an attitude that is easier to learn and describe than to maintain from day to day, especially when faced with the stress of caring for a child with serious emotional and behavioral problems. Such problems are made much worse when they are expressed while the child devalues the relationship with his parent, through rage or rejection. When a parent begins to experience blocked care, she is at risk of having great difficulty maintaining the reflective functioning and affect regulation required to remain in the open and engaged state that is central for the expression of PACE.

The first question that a social worker might ask in assessing whether or not a parent is ready to develop PACE in her relationship with her child is whether or not the parent agrees intellectually with its value. If a parent believes strongly that the behavior itself, not the relationship or the meaning of the behavior, is the important factor in influencing their child, then they are not likely to see the value of learning the attitude of PACE. Instead they will hope to rely on consequences and reinforcement patterns to influence their child. These too often lead to power struggles and increased oppositional behaviors.

The professional's initial task is to present the theory and research behind the value of secure attachments and intersubjective interactions. Neuropsychological research supports this approach. If the parent insists on the need for emphasizing behavioral consequences and not the attachment relationship, the professional might explore if she is speaking of how she was raised. Does she also believe that she should raise her child in the same manner? If she does, then emphasizing differences between her childhood and her adopted child's early years of abuse or neglect might be stressed. It may be of value to emphasize that behavioral consequences for the adoptive parents may have 'worked' because they had a relationship with their parents that was strong enough to provide a basis of trust that enabled this approach to be of value. Throughout these discussions it is crucial that the professional adopts an attitude of PACE toward the parent in order to reduce any defensiveness that might be present and to model the manner of relating that is being proposed.

Let's assume that the parent is agreeable about integrating PACE into her caregiving when she adopts a child. Will she be able to do so consistently and for an extended period of time when results (an improved relationship and behavioral functioning) are slow in coming?

One hint as to the parent's motivation to successfully utilize PACE in her interactions when she has a child is how open and engaged she is in the discussion. If she shows curiosity about the ideas presented with an eagerness to learn and an openness to try something new apart from behavioral consequences she is more likely to work to develop the necessary skills than if she is defensive. Similarly, if she conveys empathy when told how a child's fears and shame are likely to lie under his troublesome behaviors then she is more likely to be able to convey empathy toward a child who is placed with her in the future.

If the parent shows signs of defensiveness it is crucial for the professional to explore these cues, which are often nonverbal. The parent may be 'saying the right things' but with an attitude of resignation or skepticism. The professional then needs to address these nonverbal signs that suggest that the parent is truly not committed to trying a new approach but rather is agreeing to avoid a conflict. She might also feel that she has no choice but to agree with the professional who is supposed to know better than her what her child needs. The worry then would be if she is agreeing in order to ensure that the child will be placed with her, not because she truly sees the likely value of PACE.

It is also important for the professional to assess how the parent responds when any nonverbal signs of defensiveness are addressed. Does the parent openly acknowledge whatever reservations might be present and then become more engaged in the discussion? If the parent becomes open to being influenced by the professional's reasons, then she would be more likely to follow through with any commitments to try to use PACE that she makes.

Another important factor to assess is how open the parent is to relationship repair when there is a break in the relationship with the professional. If the social worker wonders if the parent is feeling judged poorly over the questions being asked, and the parent completely denies feeling annoyed though she is clearly defensive, then the professional might worry that differences in the future will not be addressed in an open manner. A much more favorable sign would be if she shows signs of increasing trust when the social worker addresses the parent's apparent guardedness, meets the social worker's concerns with openness rather than defensiveness and shows a commitment to working with the professional to repair the relationship.

If the parent has difficulty disagreeing with the therapist or acknowledging problems with implementing PACE, there is a danger that she will not successfully implement PACE. She needs to be able to trust that the alliance with the social worker is strong enough to contain differences and conflicts and failures. Honest discussions between parent and professional will be crucial if they are to successfully address their child's very challenging behaviors as an effective team.

Sometimes parents have a high motivation to utilize PACE but find it very difficult to follow through in response to certain situations, emotions or conflicts. If the parent is not willing to explore the source of this particular difficulty, then it is unlikely to be successfully managed. At times the cause is an unresolved aspect of the parent's own attachment history. While these 'triggers' are often able to be reduced when they are addressed, a parent's defensive response to addressing them can make improvement in dealing with the problem unlikely.

Another hint as to whether the parents are willing and able to utilize PACE with an adopted child is if features of PACE are evident in the relationship with each other. If the following patterns are evident in the couple's relationship, they would represent favorable signs as to their ability to demonstrate PACE with their child.

- Do the couple openly demonstrate and express warmth and affection for each other?

- Are the couple able to accept and discuss differences of opinion?

- When the couple have had a conflict were they able to address it without attacking each other, communicating a confidence that the relationship is strong enough to handle differences?

- Do the couple demonstrate an interest in and commitment to understanding the experience of each other without judgment and criticism?

- Is each partner, in turn, able to give and receive comfort and support when either one of them is experiencing distress?

The social worker might explore these five patterns both through asking how each perceives them with regard to their relationship as well as through asking for recent examples that demonstrate them.

Even more importantly, the social worker might be ready to notice the presence or absence of these patterns when various themes are discussed during the interview. If the social worker expects a certain discussion to evoke one of these patterns and it does not emerge, the social worker might comment on it and seek a response. If the parents become defensive about the resultant line of questioning, then there would be some concern that PACE might be a difficult attitude for the parent to maintain in a relationship with a child who is either oppositional or withdrawn.

Finally, the social worker needs to assess whether the parent is able to accept empathy and comfort in response to her expressions to the social worker about difficulties that she has had in her life. If she is able to demonstrate her own attachment behaviors toward the professional who is responding to her distress, she will be more likely to remain engaged in caregiving behavior toward her child in spite of his rejecting and oppositional behaviors. She will be manifesting a trusting, open and engaged relationship with the professional that will be crucial if she is to accept the professional's support in the days ahead. Whenever engaging in consistent caregiving behaviors is difficult for a parent, it is crucial that she be able to allow others to demonstrate care for her.

## Conclusion

In summary, developmental trauma, which the adopted child is at risk of manifesting, is likely to create many ongoing difficulties in attaining a successful adoption. The adopted child's attachment behaviors are likely to be seriously compromised. The adoptive parent's caregiving behaviors are likely to be seriously challenged due to a combination of her own attachment history as well as her experience of blocked care in response to her child's difficulties forming an attachment with her. A parental attitude of PACE is proposed as a means of facilitating both the parent's caregiving behaviors and her child's attachment behaviors. In order to assess the strength of a prospective adoptive placement, it is crucial that the professional is familiar with the complex challenges that parent and child may be asked to face as they engage in the often challenging process of forming a family.

## References

Cook, A., Spinazzola, J., Ford, J., Lanktree, C., Blaustein, M. and Cloitre, M. (2005) 'Complex Trauma in Children and Adolescents.' *Psychiatric Annals 35*, 5, 390–398.

Dozier, M., Stovall, C., Albus, K. and Bates, B. (2001) 'Attachment for infants in foster care: The role of caregiver state of mind.' *Child Development 72*, 1467–1477.

Golding, K. and Hughes, D. (2012) *Creating Loving Attachments*. London: Jessica Kingsley Publishers.

Hughes, D. (2009) *Attachment-Focused Parenting*. New York: W.W. Norton.

Hughes, D. and Baylin, J. (2012) *Brain-based Parenting: The Neuroscience of Caregiving for Healthy Attachment*. New York: W.W. Norton.

Lyons-Ruth, K. and Jacobvitz, D. (2008) 'Attachment Disorganization.' In J. Cassidy and P. R. Shaver (eds) *Handbook of Attachment* (2nd edition). New York: Guilford Press.

Steele, M., Hodge, J., Kaniuk, J., Hillman, S. and Henderson, K. (2003) 'Attachment representations and adoption: Associations between maternal states of mind and emotion narratives in previously maltreated children.' *Journal of Child Psychotherapy* *29*, 187–205.

CHAPTER 7

# The Parenting Brain

*Jonathan Baylin*

Parenting depends upon brain functioning and parenting well takes a lot of brain power. While all parenting is challenging, parenting non-biological children with histories of poor care may well be the most challenging kind of parenting in terms of the demands placed on brain functioning (see Box 7.1). The abilities to regulate strong emotions and to sustain good connections with another person through times of conflict depend upon brain systems that only reach maturity somewhere in our twenties. In brain terms, we are not adults until we have reached a level of brain integration that can support the ability to 'keep our lids on' under 'hot' conditions. Stress, including the stress of parenting, can suppress these 'higher' abilities even in healthy brains. So it is crucial in the assessment process to get a good sense of the health of the person's brain and how they manage stress.

Human parenting evolved from simpler mammalian caregiving processes that enable mothers (and, in some species, fathers) to shift from self-centeredness into a caregiving mode when they become parents. Humans have this core mammalian caregiving system plus 'higher' parenting powers based on the expanded brain regions that make our brains uniquely human (Bridges 2008). When we are parenting at our best, we are very fancy mammals, using both our 'bottom up' core caregiving system and our 'top down' uniquely human powers of mindsight, foresight, planning and self-regulation. These top down powers come mostly from using our prefrontal cortex (PFC) – our 'lid'. When we are parenting at our worst, we are in reactive brain states with our lids flipped, on the defensive rather than open minded and empathic, dealing with our kids 'mindlessly' rather than 'mindfully', parenting from our 'low road' (Siegel and Hartzell 2003; Hughes and Baylin 2012).

---

**BOX 7.1 ASSESSING THE PARENTING BRAIN**

In a very important sense, what we are trying to assess in prospective caregivers is their neurobiological readiness to develop and sustain a caring state of mind toward a child who is likely to be defensive toward them. While we are not putting them in a brain scanner, we can use knowledge of the parenting brain to help us explore and pay attention to the ways prospective caregivers handle their emotions, relate to significant others and deal with the conflicts that always accompany close, important relationships over time.

---

## Caregiving as a trust-building process: Helping mistrustful children feel safe

Children who come into care after being maltreated or just poorly cared for often react negatively to the efforts of well-meaning adults to get close to them. The process of trusting another person is rooted in brain functioning and the first stage of trust begins in infancy with the unconscious processing of parents' facial expressions, body language and tones of voice. Our brains detect and react to this non-verbal information within milliseconds, in less than two-tenths of a second. So we begin to trust or mistrust, feel safe or unsafe with someone, before we have any awareness that we are doing so. We don't stop using this unconscious 'people reading' system as our brain matures; we just develop 'higher', less judgmental ways of appraising the trustworthiness of others that we can use to offset the effects of our rapid judging system.

In brain terms, this means that poorly cared for children often become exquisitely sensitive to the least indications in another person's manner, especially in their facial expressions, tones of voice, body language and trustworthiness. These children's brains are so prepared to detect signs of mal-intent or rejection in others that they get many 'false alarms' from this early warning system, making them feel unsafe and causing them to react defensively, in a reflexive, 'mindless way', when in reality, there is no danger (Pollak 2003).

The process by which a child learns to trust a caregiver, then, begins very early in life and is initially orchestrated by brain systems that support implicit, unconscious information processing about other people. This fast appraisal system not only processes information, it is a learning system that makes associations between sensory information or experiences and the way these sensory experiences feel at a visceral level. These associations are then stored in the young brain as implicit, emotion-based memories of feeling safe or unsafe, experiencing pleasure or pain, in the presence of other people.

These stored associations, these memories, become the basis for anticipating how other people are going to treat us, how other people are going to react when we are close to them. Much of our brain activity is devoted to predicting what is going to happen before it actually happens and this anticipatory process is based on memories of past experiences with other people. We bring to new encounters with others our automatic expectations of what these encounters are going to be like. Only when our automatic expectations are 'violated', when the other person does not respond in the way that our brains anticipated, do we pay increased attention to what is going on. It's the novelty, the disparity between the expected experience and the actual experience, that is the trigger for new learning.

In order for these children to learn to trust an adoptive or foster parent, the adult has to be able, over time, to 'tame' these children's overactive defense systems, literally, to calm the reactivity of their hyperactive threat-detection systems. Adults who are highly approachable, warm, non-defensive and good at recovering quickly from inevitable negative reactions to people they are close to are best equipped to provide the kind of new, unexpected positive experiences that can foster the development of trust in mistrusting kids. Adults who have difficulty managing their emotions or who are very sensitive to rejection are poorly equipped for parenting challenging children (see Box 7.2).

---

**BOX 7.2 ASSESSING SENSITIVITY
TO PERCEIVED REJECTION**

Being a 'trustbuilder' as a parent depends heavily on one's tolerance for being mistrusted. This relates to a person's sensitivity to rejection. Individuals vary a lot in their sensitivity to perceived rejection and their ability to recover from self-defensive reactions to other people. People whose defensiveness is easily triggered have difficulty staying engaged in the flow of social interactions. In the interview setting, this person may exhibit signs of discomfort that interrupt the flow of discussion. Does the person show signs of 'rejection sensitivity'; that is, a tendency to take things personally when they experience tensions or conflicts with other people? Do they show some self-awareness of their own 'hot buttons', of things that trigger defensive, self-protective reactions? Ask them to talk about what 'pushes their buttons' and challenges their ability to keep caring about another person. Can they talk relatively comfortably about their own self-protective reactions or do they appear to be unfamiliar with thinking about this part of their experience? Do they show awareness of the importance of self-awareness, of knowing what makes them defensive and knowing how to manage these reactions well in close relationships?

---

# The five brain systems of parenting: Executive, approach, reward, child reading and meaning making

Parenting actually calls upon at least five different brain systems that enable us to: (1) regulate our emotions and maintain a caring state of mind toward our children; (2) stay closely engaged with our children rather than avoiding them; (3) derive pleasure and even joy from taking care of and interacting with our children; (4) understand our children's feelings and needs using our powers of empathy and 'mindsight'; and (5) construct positive narratives or stories about our children and ourselves as parents. These five systems can be called, respectively the *Executive, Approach, Reward, Child Reading* and *Meaning Making Systems* (Hughes and Baylin 2012). When a parent can access all five systems and keep them up and running over time, a child gets to interact with an open-minded, empathic, responsive adult who can be 'the grown-up in the room' when the child is being the egocentric creature that his less mature brain leads him to be. A large body of developmental neuroscience now shows that children tend to thrive when they have this 'enriched' kind of care (National Scientific Council on the Developing Child 2008).

High levels of parental stress can suppress the functioning of all five brain systems and impair the parent's ability to attune to and connect well with a child. When these systems are 'off', parents are at risk of developing 'blocked care', getting stuck in a defensive brain state that fosters more defensiveness in a child, especially a child who may have come into care already being highly mistrustful of caregivers (see Box 7.3).

---

### BOX 7.3 MULTIPLE DOMAINS OF PARENTING

In assessing prospective adoptive and foster parents, it is useful to keep this multi-domain brain-based model in mind. The interview process calls upon many of the same brain-based processes that parenting requires. Pay attention to the person's emotion regulation, 'approachability', tendency to enjoy social interaction, ability to attune to you and an adult partner as the process unfolds, and the ability to make good sense of his or her own life experiences. People who exhibit these traits in the interview are demonstrating abilities that suggest strong potential for being effective parenting figures. Pay attention to how it feels to you being with the person. Warmth and openness are 'contagious' and you will mirror these traits as you interact with a person who has them. In the same way, defensiveness and difficulty managing negative emotions are also contagious and your automatic reactions to these traits are important to be aware of.

# The neurobiology of caregiving: How we parent using bottom up and top down brain systems

We change neurobiologically when we become parents. These changes help to ensure that our priorities in life shift from more egocentric concerns to 'other care' or caregiving, to being obsessed, in a good way, with the well-being of our children. We share this chemical shifting process with all mammals. For example, female rats instinctively avoid baby rats until they have their own babies. Then, due to hormonal changes and the priming of their capacity for mothering by chemicals such as oxytocin and prolactin, the same females bond to their offspring and prefer being with them to any other 'rewarding thing' in the world, including drugs like cocaine. If these chemical changes are blocked by giving the mothers drugs that suppress oxytocin and prolactin or by stressing the mothers, they develop 'blocked care' (Martel *et al.* 1993; Bridges 2008, Hughes and Baylin 2012) and their babies start to show signs of failure to thrive. When researchers unblock the core brain systems of caregiving, the mothers resume care and infants come back to life. The same processes are at work in people, as we can see in scenarios like postpartum depression or stress-induced suppression of the capacity to care for a child.

Whether we are parenting our biological children or non-biological children, parenting well requires certain brain chemistry and circuitry to 'turn on' and stay on through good times and bad. It is the failure of these systems to work well that creates the risk for neglect and abuse.

# Staying engaged as a parent: Vagal tone and oxytocin

Parenting relies upon our *social engagement system*, a brain–body circuit that enables us to get very close to other people without getting defensive (Porges 2011). Our brains orchestrate internal shifts in our approach behavior and defensive behavior. As our brains mature, we acquire more power to manage these potentially conflicting states of mind, using both automatic, unconscious processes and top down, more conscious, executive, 'effortful' processes. While the automatic, bottom up system is working in very young brains to help children feel safe with their caregivers, the top down executive system for managing defensive reactions and staying connected to other people is only well developed in adult brains. This is why it's best to be an adult when we have children and why we have to use our adult brain powers to parent well.

The bottom up automatic process of caregiving relies heavily on brain chemicals like *oxytocin* that keep the defensive brain system from activating during close encounters between parents and children. Oxytocin receptors in the amygdala, a key brain region for switching between social engagement and self-defense, play an important part in helping parents stay close to children without becoming defensive as well as helping children trust their caregivers (Domes *et al.* 2007; Gordon *et al.* 2010). The top down brain system relies heavily on the functioning of the parent's prefrontal cortex or PFC, the region of the brain that is the slowest to mature. The PFC does not reach maturity until sometime in our twenties and is highly sensitive to the negative effects of too much stress. The ability to access the functions of the PFC in 'hot situations' is the hallmark of an adult brain, an ability that separates adults from children and teenagers, and enables a parent to be 'the grown-up in the room' when parent–child conflict occurs.

In brain terms, the ability to be a consistently nurturing parent depends heavily on brain circuitry that is tied to a part of the nervous system called the *vagus* nerve (see Porges 2011). As Dr Stephen Porges explains, primates have a branch of the vagal system that connects the heart and lungs to the muscles of the face and voice that are used to engage in social interaction without defensiveness. This 'smart vagal system' is especially developed in humans and is the neural basis for our ability to be good parents, parents who can stay open, mindful and engaged with their children over time in spite of the stresses and strains of parenthood. In fact, a fast-growing body of brain science shows that children need to interact with parents who have good vagal tone in order to develop their own potential for social engagement and self-regulation.

The vagal system travels from our digestive tract all the way up to our brain stem, connecting all regions along the way to our brains. This system is the basis for that part of our nervous system called the parasympathetic system. In contrast to the sympathetic nervous system, which ramps us up, increasing our heart rate when we need to be mobilized for action, such as in the defensive modes of fight or flight, the parasympathetic system is active when we are relaxing, digesting and being relatively immobile. The bottom parts of the vagal system orchestrate basic relaxation, digestive processes and also the freeze system that we can use for immobilized defense if we encounter an inescapable, life-threatening threat. The upper vagal system, a more recently evolved system that only exists in mammals, supports social interaction, actually making it possible, neurologically, to connect deeply with other people rather than become defensive and attack or run from them. It is this upper vagal system that is essential to good parenting.

The smart vagus not only effectively connects the lower regions of the PFC to the heart; it also links to the muscles of the face that we use to express positive emotions. This brain system also orchestrates voice quality or 'prosody', the musical quality of the voice, as exemplified in 'motherese', the way parents typically vocalize to their babies. Furthermore, Porges explains, this vagal circuit has a connection to a muscle in the inner ear that is vital to the process of listening non-defensively, tuning our hearing to the subtle sounds of emotion in human speech. This allows us to be good listeners by processing both the content of speech and the emotional qualities of each other's voices. So when a parent is using this social engagement system, she or he is in a brain state that is very conducive to connecting with and understanding a child (see Box 7.4).

## BOX 7.4 ASSESSING CAPACITY FOR STAYING ENGAGED

In the interview setting, explore the person's experiences with sustaining positive connections over time with some people in their lives. How did they deal with conflicts and what is their experience with resolving interpersonal tensions without disengaging or breaking off the relationship? Ask about a specific example of when they experienced tension in a relationship with someone they were close to. What do they think caused the tension? How did they feel as this was happening in the relationship? What did they think the other person was feeling and thinking? How did this turn out? What did they do to try to resolve the conflict? The goal here is to assess the person's ability to think 'relationally', not just egocentrically, to take the other person's perspective, to empathize, especially when there is tension in the relationship.

Ask about experiences with children, such as babysitting, coaching and mentoring, and inquire about how the person experienced these relationships emotionally. In particular, how did they handle situations where they had to correct a child? Were they able to combine 'connection with correction', staying mindful of the child's feelings at the same time that they were firm with the child about a rule or acceptable behavior? Did they enjoy these relationships? Do they exhibit some warmth and pleasure as they recall these experiences? Also, pay attention to your own reactions to being with the person. Does the person smile and make it comfortable to be near him or her? These are signs of the kind of approachability, warmth and good vagal tone that an adopted or foster child would sense and that would help these children to begin to feel safe in care.

The flip side here is to inquire about stress, both historically and currently, since stress can suppress the higher functions needed to parent well. Ask about their current stressors and how they see themselves coping with them. How would they see themselves handling the additional stress of parenting a child who may come with 'issues'?

## Developing the brain potential for parenting: Genes and early life experiences

When it comes to the development of potential for caregiving, life is not fair. It is simply true that people who come into the world with certain genes and then receive very good care early in life are more likely to become very good parents later in life than people who come into the world with 'risky' genes and then receive poor care early in life. The combination of (1) genes that tend to confer resilience or that buffer people from the negative effects of stress, and (2) being well nurtured early in life is now known to promote healthy brain development and to promote the development of a well-connected brain that supports good emotion regulation, empathy and the ability to sustain a caring state of mind under stress (Beuregard, Levesque and Bourgouin 2001; Cushing and Kramer 2005; Cozolino 2006).

It is not just a coincidence that the descriptions of healthy brain functioning and of the characteristics of adults with secure attachment styles are basically identical. New research is revealing that different attachment styles in adults reflect different levels of neural integration, differences in brain development. So when we speak of the brain powers needed to parent well we are also talking about an adult's attachment status (see Box 7.5). Adults who have a secure style of adult attachment, called 'autonomous', are now known to have good neural integration. So there is a strong relationship between assessing an adult's attachment status and assessing the health of their brains (van IJzendoorn 1995; Strathearn and Fonagy 2009).

---

**BOX 7.5 EXPLORING ATTACHMENT HISTORIES**

One of the major implications for assessment of potential adopters and fosterers is the importance of exploring their attachment histories – their early experiences with their own caregivers. It is important, then, to inquire in the assessment process about these early experiences. What's important here is not the experiences themselves, but how the person currently makes sense of these experiences. There are two basic ways that an adult can acquire a secure attachment style: from being well nurtured as a child during the formative stage for attachment, and from working through and resolving the negative effects of poor care later in life through a combination of exposure to a safe, trusting relationship and hard work facing and processing 'the bad stuff' from early life. In brain terms, both of these routes to inner security involve the strengthening of connections between the higher regions of the brain, the PFC, and the lower, more primitive, more reflexive regions of the brain often referred to as the limbic system. The stronger these connections, the better able a person is to regulate his or her own emotions, to think clearly about relational processes, to understand him or herself and to sustain an empathic state of mind toward 'significant others'.

---

# Parental reward system: Getting pleasure and satisfaction from parenting

Beyond feeling safe enough to be very close to a child, it is important that parents experience some joy and satisfaction from the process of raising children. The parental reward system is based on the brain chemistry and anatomy that trigger positive emotions in response to things in life that are important for our survival, including good relationships with other people. The reward system in the brain depends heavily upon the chemical, dopamine. All things 'rewarding' in life, from the social pleasures of companionship and parenting to taking illicit drugs like cocaine, depend upon activation of dopamine.

When people are struggling to find any pleasure in life or to feel motivated to engage with life, there is usually a problem with dopamine functioning, as in depression. In the parenting domain, dopamine is released when parents interact with their children in playful, enjoyable ways and this release of dopamine helps to sustain the caregiving process and to make positive memories of experiences with parenting. While oxytocin primes the parenting process, dopamine helps to maintain it (Fleming *et al.* 2008).

There is an immediate reward system that is activated by a child's positive responses to parental care, such as the irresistible smiles of a four-month-old baby. In adults, there is also a capacity to use the reward system to derive pleasure and satisfaction from pursuing and achieving long-term goals that require self-regulation, self-monitoring and perseverance, such as the goal of being a caring parent of a challenging child. When, for whatever reason, a child isn't able to provide the kinds of reciprocal responses that are immediately rewarding, parenting is inevitably more challenging. Parenting children in care who are deeply mistrustful often requires that the parents use the more goal-driven reward system while managing their reactions to the lack of immediate gratification. For example, when a parent can take pride in managing the challenges of staying open and non-defensive with a defensive child, this can provide a deeper kind of reward than the more immediate, automatic rewards of interacting with a child who easily reciprocates the parent's love. The parent's ability to manage their reward system and avoid the negative effects of dashed expectations for immediate reward from children is a crucial aspect of adoptive and foster care (see Boxes 7.6 and 7.7).

## BOX 7.6 ASSESSING CAPACITY FOR PLAYFULNESS

In the interview, explore the person's capacity for enjoying social interaction and for being playful. Ask about their most enjoyable experiences with others and pay attention to signs of having a sense of humor. In a sense, the goal is to assess the person's potential to help a child to experience being a source of pleasure, even, hopefully, a source of delight, an experience that many children coming into care have never had. The ability to find ways to enjoy a child who may be highly defensive requires a willingness to engage in a wide range of activities, some of which may be out of the adult's comfort zone at first. An adult with a narrow range of interests may have difficulty finding ways to 'meet a child where he's at' to create mutually enjoyable experiences.

## BOX 7.7 ASSESSING CAPACITY TO PURSUE LONG-TERM PARENTING GOALS

Another important aspect of the parental reward system to assess is the ability to derive satisfaction from working on long-term goals as opposed to needing immediate gratification. Parenting well requires the ability to tolerate a lack of immediate rewards when a child does not easily respond in positive ways to the parent's caring behavior. The ability to set longer-term goals such as helping a mistrustful child learn to trust over time rests upon the parent's ability to take pleasure in doing a good job of being patient and celebrating small steps in the child's ability to trust. Parents need to adjust their expectations about a child's ability to reciprocate love so that they don't experience the crash of their reward system when their expectations keep being dashed. Ask about the person's experiences with handling disappointments. Inquire about their experiences with pursuing goals over time, when they were not experiencing immediate, short-term rewards.

## Parental child reading system

There is great variability among parents in their capacity for tuning in to a child's inner experiences to see 'underneath' a child's behavior and understand what a child may be experiencing. This is a brain process that is highly dependent on the functioning of the right hemisphere, which specializes in processing non-verbal communication and picking up signals from facial expressions, prosody and body language. Very left brained, highly logical parents who have difficulty with non-verbal aspects of communication often find it hard to attune to their children's inner life and to develop a richly 'intersubjective' relationship with a child.

Also, high levels of stress can interfere with this 'mindsight' process, narrowing a parent's attention to a child in a ways that promote a strictly behavioral, corrective stance toward the child while suppressing parental empathy and compassion (see Box 7.8). Fortunately, recent research into the brain processes involved in 'people reading' or mindsight shows that in most people, it is probably possible to improve in this area of parental functioning with the right kinds of practice (Mascaro *et al.* 2013).

---

**BOX 7.8 ASSESSING MINDSIGHT**

The interview setting provides opportunities to observe the person's ability to tune in to your non-verbal communication as well as that of an adult partner. People who have difficulty with 'people reading' or mindsight may not pick up subtle feedback that they are getting off track or talking too much. They may have difficulty answering questions about feelings and responding to questions that require some introspection and self-awareness. Does the person monitor the flow of the interview and make adjustments to stay on track, or do you find yourself having to work hard to refocus the discussion and keep things from wandering too much?

---

## Parental meaning making system: Making good sense of a child's behavior and experiences of being a parent

The parental meaning making system involves the way that an adult makes sense of a child's often confusing behavior and the complicated experiences of being a parent. Parents who are able to 'get their minds around' the often conflicting experiences of raising children to construct positive narratives about their children and about their role as parents are better able to sustain the kind of positive, compassionate, engaged state of mind that is conducive to children's development. This can be very challenging when parenting children who have difficulty reciprocating love and making their parents feel delighted by their presence. Since children entering care are likely to have some degree of blocked trust and defensiveness, adopters and foster carers have to be able to make sense of these children's approach/avoidance behavior in ways that prevent the construction of very negative narratives, such as stories of having an ungrateful, 'bad kid' or of being a failure as a parent (see Box 7.9).

---

### BOX 7.9 ASSESSING CAPACITY FOR INTEGRAIVE THINKING

An important aspect of the process of constructing meaning from experiences as a parent is the ability to understand a child's conflicted behavior toward care, the frequent approach/ avoidance conflict that mistrusting children exhibit. Parents' ability to 'get their mind around' the seeming contradictions in these children's behavior and to make sense of seeming opposites rather than getting stuck in black and white thinking is a key aspect of parenting mistrusting children. Under stress, it is hard to engage in this kind of integrative thinking.

Ask about times when the person has been confused about something and how they tried to make sense of the confusion. Have there been times in their relationships when their own reactions to someone they love confused them and made them wonder why they could have strong negative feelings about someone they cared about? How did they try to make sense of these conflicting feelings and thoughts? Were they able to resolve the confusion in a helpful way, or did the internal conflict lead to blame or shame?

## Conclusion

All aspects of parenting are based, ultimately, on brain functioning. Parenting children who come from poor care requires a healthy brain. Think of the assessment process as a stress test for gathering information about the health of the person's brain. Assessment should include exploration of the person's approachability and capacity for executive functioning, both bottom up and top down brain functions. It is especially important to assess the person's ability to regulate negative emotions and defensive reactions, executive functions that depend upon the prefrontal power to keep your lid on in hot situations. Look for evidence of the ability to read non-verbal communication well since parenting depends heavily on this right brain capacity. Get a sense of the person's potential to enjoy children, including their tendency to be playful. Also, inquire about their ability to get satisfaction from less immediately rewarding things in life, including doing something well. Finally, history matters when it comes to parenting, so explore prospective caregivers' experiences with their own attachment figures and with adult relationships, paying attention to how they make sense of these relationships and how well they seem to have dealt with challenging aspects of growing up and sustaining connections with significant others.

## References

Beuregard, M., Levesque, J. and Bourgouin, P. (2001) 'Neural correlates of conscious self-regulation of emotion.' *Journal of Neuroscience 21*, 1–6.

Bridges, R. (ed.) (2008) *Neurobiology of the Parental Brain*. San Diego, CA: Academic Press.

Cozolino, L. (2006) *The Neuroscience of Human Relationships*. New York: W.W. Norton.

Cushing, B.S. & Kramer,K.M. (2005) 'Mechanisms underlying epigenetic effects of early social experience: The role of neuropeptides and steroids.' *Neuroscience and Biobehavioral Reviews 29*, 1089–1105.

Domes, G., Heinrichs, M., Glascher, J., Buchel, C., Braus, D. F. and Herpetz, S. C. (2007) 'Oxytocin attenuates amygdala responses to emotional faces regardless of valence.' *Biological Psychiatry 10*, 1187–1190.

Fleming, A. S., Gonazalez, A., Afonso, V. and Lovic, V. (2008) 'Plasticity in the Maternal Neural Circuit: Experience, Dopamine and Mothering.' In R. Bridges (ed.) *Neurobiology of the Parental Brain*. San Diego, CA: Academic Press.

Gordon, H., Zagoory-Sharon, O., Leckman, J.F. and Feldman, R. (2010) 'Oxytocin and the development of parenting in humans.' *Biological Psychiatry 68*, 377–382.

Hughes, D. and Baylin, J. (2012) *Brain-based Parenting*. New York: W.W. Norton.

Martel, F. L., Nevison, C. M., Raymon, F. D., Simpson, M. J. A. and Keverne, E. B. (1993) 'Opioid receptor blockade reduces maternal affect and social grooming in rhesus monkeys.' *Psychoneuroimmunology 18*, 307–321.

Mascaro, J.S., Rilling, J.K., Negi, L.T. and Raison, C.L. (2013) 'Compassion meditation enhances empathic accuracy and related neural activity.' *Social Cognitive and Affective Neuroscience 8 (1)*, 48–55.

National Scientific Council on the Developing Child (2008) *The Timing and Quality of Early Experiences Combine to Shape Brain Architecture*. Center on the Developing Child, Harvard University, Working Paper 5.

Pollak, S. D. (2003) 'Experience-dependent Affective Learning and Risk for Psychopathology in Children.' In R. King, C. F. Ferris and I. L. Lederhendlerk (eds) *Roots of Mental Illness in Children*. New York: New York Academy of Sciences.

Porges, S. (2011) *The Polyvagal Theory: Neurophysiological Foundations of Emotions, Attachment, Communication, and Self-regulation.* New York: W.W. Norton.

Strathearn, L. and Fonagy, P. (2009) 'Adult attachment predicts maternal brain and oxytocin response to infant cues.' *Neuropsychopharmacology 34*, 2655–2666.

Van IJzendoorn, M. (1995) 'Adult attachment representations, parental responsiveness, and infant attachment.' *Psychological Bulletin 117*, 3, 387–403.

# CHAPTER 8

# Reflective Functioning and Parenting

*Jonathan Baylin*

The ability to tolerate experiences of being mistrusted by a child without losing compassion for the child goes to the heart of adoptive and foster care for mistreated children. A crucial aspect of parenting is the ability to step back from negative emotional reactions toward a child and engage in the slower and deeper mental process called reflection. *Reflective functioning* enables a parent to use 'mindsight' (Siegel 2010), the ability to tune in to a child's feelings and to take the child's perspective in order to better understand what is motivating the child's behavior.

Reflective functioning enables parents to think relationally about their interactions with their children rather than reacting to the child's behavior egocentrically. Reflective functioning helps parents shift their mental stance toward a child from their 'low road' self-protective reactions to the 'high road' process that we use to 'get a grip', to come to our senses. Engaging in reflection enables us to put intense emotional experiences in perspective, to make better sense of our own and our child's reactions, and to learn from our experiences how to be a better parent. We need to access our high road thinking in order to understand and empathize with someone who has hurt us, especially when that person is in our care and we are committed to being a good caregiver. When we activate this mental high road, we can think with feeling, combining the processes of mentalization or 'mind reading' with empathy to enhance our understanding of, and compassion for, ourselves and others (Fonagy *et al.* 2002).

Parents need to use their reflective capacity in order to stay parental, to be the grown up in the relationship. In a very important sense, reflective functioning is the key to parents being able to value their relationship with a child over the need to correct the child's behavior in the moment. In the heat of negative interactions with a child, the natural tendency is to hyper-focus on the child's behavior, losing the ability, temporarily, to empathize with the child. While children need parental guidance, this guidance is most effective when the child feels safe with the parent and trusts the parent's intentions. Reflective functioning supports parents' ability to put 'connection over correction' in their overall approach to parenting, a form of parenting that helps children to feel understood, lessen their defensiveness and eventually make the desired journey from mistrust to trust. A growing body of research, including brain imaging studies of parents, reveals strong connections between parents' reflective functioning, their attachment style, their attentiveness to children's needs and their children's attachment style (Strathearn and Fonagy 2009).

## Reflection and the brain

When we are in reflective mode, we use our brains quite differently than we do when we are in self-protective, egocentric mode. In brain science terms, egocentric is not a pejorative or negative term; it refers to a form of information processing that engages the lower or ventral stream of the brain rather than the higher or dorsal stream. Since the ventral stream is strongly connected to the body, this is the brain system we use when we experience life with immediacy and 'take things personally'. In fact, it is part of the job of this lower brain system to rapidly assess all experiences for their personal relevance, for their immediate emotional importance, to help us stay safe. When this ventral stream is overactive, it is difficult to distinguish between experiences that are 'personal' and those that are not. In the extreme, intense activation of the ventral stream in combination with underactivation of the dorsal stream, which helps to 'contextualize' experiences, creates deep mistrust, even paranoia.

The lower, faster brain system has the job of quickly assessing the trustworthiness and approachability of other people. This system does not take the time to make fine distinctions between one person and another. Its job is not to dither, not to deal with complexity and nuance. It is actually the task of this brain system to do the thing we are often cautioned not to do: to judge the book quickly by its cover. The rapid appraisal process evolved to categorize, to stereotype, to get a quick read on another person as a first step in knowing whether to approach or avoid that person. As a key aspect of this quick appraisal process, the amygdala on the right side of our brains has been shown to react within 50 milliseconds to the color of someone's skin, their age, their gender, their facial expression, their tone of voice – even the amount of white displayed in their eyes, as in facial expressions of fear and surprise. In short, this system works by over-generalizing from very rudimentary information to rapidly categorizing information about another person for a 'first take' on their trustworthiness, approachability and safety (Davis and Whalen 2001).

Not concerned with being 'right', the motto of this speedy appraisal system is 'better safe than sorry'. It is not the brain system we use to make impartial, objective assessments about other people or to develop compassion for people who are very different from us or who treat us poorly. This is not the brain system that enables us to take the high road, to 'love our enemies', to understand people who mistrust us. That's the work of 'higher' brain regions that work much more slowly, in brain time, than the core survival-oriented system whose job is to keep us alive in the moment. As a result of the speed and roughness of these first appraisals, we are initially very judgmental and we can easily be misled by this system regarding another person's intentions. This is especially true when this system has been sensitized by exposure to untrustworthy caregivers, forcing a child's brain to become expert at detecting the signs of threat in others within milliseconds.

When we reflect, we use the middle regions of the prefrontal cortex, or MPFC, a place in the brain where the lower and higher processing streams converge. This region of the brain, which is uniquely human in its size compared to our fellow species, receives input from all of the regions of the brain involved in processing our experiences with other people, and brings all of this information to bear on the process of understanding both self and other (Frith and Frith 2003).

The MPFC does not reach full functional maturity until sometime in the twenties. In brain terms, this is why adults have much more capacity for reflection than children and why parenting in adulthood is different in important ways from parenting as a teen. The MPFC is a part of our 'lid', so when we flip our lids in the heat of emotionally intense interpersonal situations, we lose the ability to reflect, becoming, for the moment, more childlike in our brain functioning. When this happens, children lose the presence of a grown up in the room, creating the potential for mutual defensiveness and mindless conflict.

## Reflective functioning and compassion toward self and child

Reflective functioning helps a parent to sustain a compassionate state of mind toward herself or himself and toward a child whose behavior is challenging. When a parent can maintain a caring, compassionate mindset toward the child, the child is more likely to feel accepted and safe being close to the parent. In a very real sense, compassion is contagious; unfortunately, so is defensiveness. Compassion competes with our self-protective reactions and only arises when we step back from our egocentric perspective. We have to make space in our brains for compassion to arise; it doesn't emerge automatically and it is blocked by self-defensive operations (Mascaro et al. 2013). Compassion is an open brain state in which we can approach the object of our compassion with our minds ready to learn from our experiences. If the suppression of a parent's reflective capacity becomes chronic, the parent is virtually unable to grow as a parent, to use experiences of parenting to keep getting better at being a parent.

Parenting inevitably triggers reactions in us that we may have never experienced before, especially if we are generally calm, loving people. Getting intensely angry with a child you are 'supposed to love' can be very unsettling for kind people and can lead to feelings of shame or guilt. Being able to step back from intense emotional reactions to reflect on what one is experiencing as a parent can help to resolve the internal conflict between one's goal to be a loving parent and the inevitable unloving feelings that get triggered by being 'up close and personal' with a child who, in that moment, is not feeling at all loving toward us. Using the reflective process to resolve these conflicts constructively can prevent a parent from developing chronic shame or guilt and from disengaging from a child emotionally in order to protect themself from feelings of shame. Reflective functioning, in short, helps to prevent parental 'blocked care' (Hughes and Baylin 2012) (see Box 8.1).

---

### BOX 8.1 THE PARENTING HIGH ROAD

The ability to shift from an egocentric perspective to a reflective mode is especially important in parenting a child who comes into care with a history of poor treatment and an insecure, mistrusting attachment style. Applied to the assessment process, it is important to evaluate a prospective caregiver's ability to 'take the high road' when someone they are close to misconstrues their intentions or hurts their feelings. Ask questions about how the person has handled it when someone they are close to has mistrusted them or hurt their feelings. Throughout the interview, pay attention to the person's tendency to stop and think in response to your questions rather than responding quickly, without reflection.

---

## Reflective functioning and the management of social pain: It's not personal

Having loving intentions misconstrued by a child as bad intentions is a powerful trigger for what brain scientists call 'social pain': the very real pain of rejection. Recent brain research shows that hurt feelings activate essentially the same brain circuitry as physical pain. In brain terms, 'pain is pain', whether it is a sore leg or sore feelings (Lieberman 2012). When we experience either kind of pain, physical or social/emotional, our brains try to protect us from suffering by activating a pain suppression system to keep the pain at bay. This system involves the automatic release of pain suppressing chemicals, most importantly, the class of brain chemicals called opioids. The same regions of the brain that have to be 'on' in order for a parent to feel caring and loving toward a child are also regions that are very rich in opioid receptors. This enables us to adjust or 'titrate' our level of caring and to suppress the pain of having our feelings hurt. In brain terms, this is why 'love hurts' and why we have to have a way to control social pain. What can easily happen, then, in the parenting brain when a child rejects the parent's efforts to get close to the child, to enter the child's 'personal space', is that the pain of being rebuffed can trigger the automatic pain suppression system, which does two things at once: (1) it dulls the pain of feeling rejected, and (2) it suppresses the parent's ability to care for the child, to value the child, literally turning off the parental care system and causing at least temporary blocked care.

The process of sorting out the personal from the non-personal is a vital part of reflective functioning. When we reflect on 'hot' moments of parenting later, in a quieter state of mind, we can use the reflective process to ask ourselves 'Does Jimmy really just hate and disrespect me or was he having a bad day and told me to go to hell because his lid was flipped and he had momentary blocked care? Hmmm, since I know what it's like when I get very angry and flip my lid, I guess he was just doing what I do when I lose it and say things I don't really, truly, mean. I think I'll go let him know that I'm sorry I took it so personally and that I hope he has a better day tomorrow.'

## Reflective functioning and integrative thinking: Minding the whole child

Reflective functioning enables parents to remember and value what they have learned about the effects of poor care on children's development, how their adopted or foster child developed blocked trust in the first place. The process of reflection deepens your relationship with whatever you reflect upon. For example, if you reflect on your child's feelings rather than your child's actions, you deepen your awareness and understanding of your child's inner experience. In a sense, reflection is like a laser beam that you shine on a certain aspect of your life and by doing so, change the way you look at, feel about and value that aspect. So reflective functioning is a deepening, enriching process that strengthens your ability to understand and attune to the 'object of your reflection'. Reflecting about your child changes your relationship with the child in your mind, in the mental space where you hold the image of the child. This is why Siegel and Bryson in their book, *The Whole-Brain Child* (2011) and Dan Hughes (2007) in his dyadic developmental model of parenting, place so much emphasis on the parent's reflective process. Parental reflection about a child strengthens the parent's ability to maintain a more holistic, multi-dimensional, integrated image or mental model of the child to use as a template or schema for guiding the way the parent relates to the child.

One of the goals of reflective functioning is to be able to see how two things that at first appear to be opposites and that just don't make sense together actually are part of a larger picture in which they do go together. For example, experiencing a mistrusting child's approach and avoidance behavior towards us can seem confusing, making no sense. But when we are able to step back from the egocentric state and reflect on our child's behavior, we can start to see how the approach/avoidance pattern is part of a larger pattern of blocked trust and makes sense based on this concept.

By using reflection, the parent 'can get her mind around' seemingly opposite parts of the child, including the sweet part and the angry, oppositional, defensive part. When the parent can construct an integrated 'working model' of the child that embraces all of the child rather than taking a 'black and white' polarizing stance toward the child, the parent is literally constructing an internal representation of the child that can promote the same integrative process in the child. In other words, when the parent can construct this integrative, coherent model of the child, this model then becomes the basis for relating to the child in a more empathic, holistic, integrated way, in a way that the child will 'feel', will sense and will mirror. This mirroring of the parent's holistic, accepting, compassionate way of relating can promote psychological integration in the child, helping a child develop emotional resilience, empathy and positive self-esteem.

This ability to shift from polarized or black-and-white thinking to integrated thinking in which black and white can go together is extremely important for parenting well. Under stress, we tend to get stuck in either-or mode and can't see the 'bigger picture' or the forest for the trees. While we inevitably engage in this kind of 'knowing' when we have strong emotional reactions to anything in life, we have to be able to disengage from this brain state, to let go of this rapid judging, quick appraisal state, in order to deal with our child more thoughtfully and compassionately.

Since this kind of higher, more integrative thinking is tied to brain maturation, it is the parent who has to 'go there' because the child, having a less mature brain, is much less capable of making this kind of brain shift, much more likely to be stuck in black and white, egocentric, either-or mind states. This is especially true of children who had to devote their earliest brain development to living defensively, a process that later makes it harder for them to stop reacting habitually to caregivers as if they are a threat. Indeed, experts in the field of reflective functioning and attachment believe that it is essential for a child to be able to interact with a caregiver who has the capacity for reflection in order for the child to make the shift from automatic mistrust to trust (Fonagy *et al.* 2002; Hughes 2007).

## Reflective functioning and intersubjectivity

The MPFC reflection system is crucial for engaging in *intersubjective* relationships: relationships that incorporate and value an awareness of, and interest in, each other's mental/emotional life. Research in the field of social neuroscience shows that intersubjective relationships between parents and children are vital to healthy child development, essential for promoting neural integration in children, especially the kind of brain development that supports the processes of social engagement, empathy, resilience and capacity for parenting later in life (National Scientific Council on the Developing Child 2008, 2010). When parents attune to the inner experiences of their children and use this knowledge to understand their children better, the parents are providing enriched care, the kind of care that is radically different from maltreatment and neglect, the kind of care that gives a defensive child a chance to learn to feel safe with a trustworthy adult.

# Reflective functioning, personal safety and stress

Reflective functioning requires shifting your attention from the outside world and going inside for a while; it's an inherently introspective process. So to reflect, you have to feel safe enough, internally as well as externally, to go inside in this way, to take your eyes off your external environment and to face your internal thoughts and feelings. When you have a negative self-concept, believing that you are of low value, the process of thinking about yourself and your relationships can be painful, making it very difficult to 'go there' and reflect. Instead of reflecting productively, the person with low self-esteem is more likely to ruminate, perseverating on negative thoughts, or to avoid the process altogether to avoid painful, negative feelings.

Reflection requires the ability to catch yourself wandering into negative places and bringing yourself back to the reflective process. In this way, reflection is a form of mindfulness, a process similar to what we are doing with our brains when we meditate: focusing on the breath, catching the wanderings, and coming back to the breath. In the case of reflective functioning, instead of focusing on the breath, you are focusing on the relational processes and minding both yourself and your child.

Perhaps the most powerful use of reflective functioning is following negative, upsetting experiences with a child, especially situations when the parent 'lost it', took things too personally and got stuck in a defensive reaction. This is when it is especially important for the parent to be able to step back later and revisit the 'hot' scenario with a cooler mind and take a deeper look at what happened and why. Parents who are chronically stressed out, sometimes since childhood, may not have enough 'inner safety', safety with their own thoughts and feelings, to engage in self-reflection. Reflection is an introspective process that requires shifting your attention from outside to inside, literally taking your mind off what is going on in your environment in order to focus inwardly on memories, prior knowledge and internal states.

Stress, then, can impede the ability to shift from self-defense to reflective functioning. In a chronically stressed parent, the reflective process may not activate automatically, leaving the parent stuck in the more egocentric state of mind in which she continues to feel mistreated by her child, to take the child's behavior personally. Without accessing her reflective functioning, this parent is at the mercy of her self-defensive mind and is likely to disengage from her child and experience more chronic blocked care. The parent's ability to manage stress and to resolve the lingering effects of early life stress are important aspects of keeping the brain healthy enough to engage the reflective process and not get mired in self-defensiveness.

## Reflection, reappraisal and the process of changing your mind

Reflection is connected to another brain-based process called reappraisal (Banfield *et al.* 2004). This involves the process of changing your beliefs about important things in life based on reassessment of old beliefs in the light of new information and knowledge. In the parenting realm, this is an extremely important mental capacity because parenting requires that we update our beliefs about parenting and about our child based on both new experiences that we reflect upon and new information that we learn from a variety of sources.

Reflective functioning can pave the way or 'prime' the process of reappraisal, a process that depends on a higher brain region called the dorsal lateral prefrontal cortex (DLPFC), which lies above the MPFC region that appears to orchestrate the process of reflection. When reflection leads to awareness that old beliefs are in conflict with new information, the DLPFC provides the brain space for 'conflict resolution', where the old and new ways of thinking give way to a new paradigm or cognitive framing that either replaces the old or integrates the old and the new (Banfield *et al.* 2004).

So, for example, if the parent has the longstanding belief that children should be seen and not heard and then is exposed to new information that being seen and heard promotes children's brain development, that parent may reflect upon these two ways of thinking, experience the tension of the disparity between them and, by staying with this process, engage the DLPFC conflict resolution process to resolve the conflict, hopefully in favor of embracing the newer way of thinking about raising children. In this scenario, the parent is using the higher, uniquely human brain processes of reflection and reappraisal to resolve internal conflicts in a flexible, adaptive way, changing her mind to attune better to the needs of a developing child.

## Parental attachment status and reflective functioning

Parents who have unresolved memories of painful, frightening or shaming experiences are prone to being triggered by their interactions with their children into 'unparental' states of mind during which they lose touch with what is really happening in the parent–child relationship in the moment. These parental 'disappearances' or 'out of the blue' emotional reactions are inevitably dysregulating to a child and can even be traumatizing (Tronick 2007).

Unfairly, then, parents who grow up in environments that are very stressful and that engender strong feelings of fear are likely to have more sensitive defense systems than parents who grow up in safety. Early childhood is a time when the brain is learning about the nature of interpersonal relationships and is also getting 'tuned' to a certain level of reactivity or sensitivity to different kinds of social situations and especially to the non-verbal communication that signals approachability or threat in others. Parents from unsafe childhoods are likely to experience limbic reactions to their children that are inconsistent with their intentions as parents. Implicit defensive reactions caused by limbic 'false alarms' can make it very difficult for a parent to stay open, present and attuned to a child in the moment. This is one of the most powerful reasons why we say that parent development begins in early childhood with the type of caregiving environment available to the parent-in-the-making (Teicher et al. 2003).

Parents who have a secure style of adult attachment can use reflective functioning more easily and productively than parents who have unresolved attachments, dismissive attachments, or preoccupied attachments (Strathearn and Fonagy 2009). The insecure attachment styles involve either suppression of attachment-related feelings and thoughts, preoccupation with and rumination about these feelings and thoughts, or trauma-based lack of emotional safety with these feelings and thoughts. This is why it is important for parents who have insecure attachment styles to work on developing a more secure style (see Box 8.2).

---

**BOX 8.2 PARENT'S HOT BUTTONS**

In assessment terms, we need to consider a potential caregiver's openness to exploring their own attachment history and attachment style. Parenting inevitably triggers the parent's 'hot buttons', those things about ourselves that we haven't yet resolved sufficiently from the past to be able to stay regulated when these issues come up. Ask the person to talk about their hot buttons and about how they would try to deal with being triggered by a child. Being aware of these triggers and being willing to work at defusing them is a very important dimension of someone's potential for parenting challenging children.

---

## Strengthening the ability to reflect: New research on the brain-building power of reflective functioning

A hot new area of brain research is revealing that the practice of reflection, as in meditative and mindfulness practices, promotes the growth of brain fibers and strengthens connections in the MPFC region of the brain, the region that appears to support reflective functioning (Chielsa and Serretti 2010; Tang *et al.* 2012; Mascaro *et al.* 2013). To be very specific, the MPFC connects with a region of the brain just behind it that is part of the cingulate. This front part of the cingulate has fibers that connect it to the MPFC and when these two regions are strongly connected it is easier to reflect, to engage in reflective thinking, introspection. This is the vital connection that appears to grow and be strengthened by reflective practice.

Intriguingly, this brain system is turned on when we are engaging in compassionate thoughts about ourselves and about other people.

In contrast, this brain system is actually found to be smaller in people who have a negative view of themselves, who consider themselves to be 'of low rank'. In short, this reflective brain system appears to be important for being compassionate and accepting toward ourselves and towards others, and using this brain system by engaging in 'compassion meditation' appears to make it stronger. Amazingly, we can apparently make ourselves more compassionate, empathic and patient by building up this brain region through using it (see *Annals of the New York Academy of Sciences*, Volume 1307, 2014 for a recent review).

## Assessing reflective functioning in potential adopters

Given the importance of reflective functioning to prevent the onset of blocked care in an adoptive parent, the assessment of reflective functioning in the evaluation process is an essential component of the overall process of making a decision about a prospective adopter's capacity for helping an adopted or foster child form a secure attachment. People vary greatly in reflectiveness, partly genetically and partly due to life experiences and brain development. If someone is under great stress, they will have difficulty being reflective and probably will have an underdeveloped reflective system. People on the autism spectrum and people with non-verbal processing difficulties have problems with reflective functioning and mindsight, not due just to stress, but due to wiring problems in their brains. People with unresolved traumatic memories have difficulty being reflective because the reflective process brings up the bad memories in a way that is 'too hot to handle' and this shuts off the reflective process.

While there are structured procedures used in research to assess reflective functioning, it is quite possible in a relatively brief interview context to get a reading on a person's tendency to engage in self-reflection. Certain personality traits, such as 'openness' and 'flexibility' are consistent with reflective functioning and, in effect, show that a person is able to reflect. People who show curiosity in an interview, who are open to new ideas and seem interested in learning from their experiences are likely to have good reflective functioning because reflection is a close cousin of curiosity and an openness to learning.

An assessor can get a good impression of a prospective caregiver's reflective functioning from aspects of the interaction during an interview. When a person has these underlying brain functions, he or she is able to stay engaged during the assessment, to keep from becoming defensive and to exhibit a capacity for curiosity and thoughtfulness. In a way, the interview situation is a stress test and people who exhibit resilience, flexibility and openness in this setting are likely to have good reflective capacity.

In the interview setting, the interviewer could inquire about the process a person uses to deal with situations in which their feelings get hurt. The evaluator could ask, for example:

- How would you see yourself handling situations when your adopted child hurt your feelings by resisting your care?

- How do you handle hurt feelings in your relationship with your partner?

- People differ a lot in their sensitivity to rejection. Where do you see yourself in this regard and what kinds of interactions with a child would be most challenging to you in this respect?

You could also inquire about the person's own history of times when they have had to deal with rejection or relationship break ups, since the ability to handle rejection is so vital for adoptive and foster parents. How does the interviewee respond? Do they exhibit some reflective capacity as they talk about these kinds of hurtful experiences or do they struggle with this aspect of their life experience? What you are looking for here is a capacity to be open about having been hurt at times and the ability to reflect on these experiences rather than being stuck in hurt feelings.

## Priming reflective functioning in an assessment setting

The assessor can also use specific questions that require reflective capacity in the interview process. For example, Daniel Siegel, in his latest book, *Brainstorm* (2014), provides a list of such questions. Here are some questions mostly adapted from the ones Siegel suggests:

- What was your parents' philosophy about raising children?

- Would you parent in a similar way, or differently? Why?

- How have your relationships in your family changed over time?

- Have you had any significant losses in your life? If so, what impact has this had on you?

- How do you communicate with others when your feelings are running high?

- Are there supportive relationships you can rely on when things get stressful and you can use some help?

- Did you feel secure as a child to go out and explore the world?

- How do you imagine the experiences from your childhood may shape the way you would parent an adopted or foster child?

- How do you think you might handle it if a child was having difficulty learning to trust you?

The purpose of these kinds of questions is to get a sense of the person's ability to engage in reflective, relational thinking. How comfortable does the person seem with being introspective and recalling his or her own relational experiences? Is there resistance to engaging in this process? If the person seems to be able to reflect, what is the nature of what they 'produce' from reflecting? What's important here is not so much the content of what they say but how well they are able to make sense of their past experiences. In research on reflective function using a structured interview process such as the Adult Attachment Interview (AAI), the goal is to see how 'coherent' the person's narrative is when he or she talks about childhood experiences with attachment figures. No matter what those experiences were, even if they were traumatic, if the person can produce a coherent narrative and can tell the story of their early life experiences including the good, the bad and the ugly, without becoming emotionally dysregulated, this is a strong indicator that the person has good reflective functioning and a secure adult attachment style.

# Reflective functioning and parental 'hot buttons'

In a book about parental emotion regulation, Bonnie Harris (*When Your Kids Push Your Buttons and What You Can Do About It*, 2003) describes 10 different 'hot buttons' common to parents. These could be used in an interview setting to ask prospective adopters which of these they are most likely to experience. This can be part of the process of assessing the person's capacity for reflection and self-awareness and openness versus defensiveness. The 'hot buttons' include:

- the approval button
- the control button
- the appreciation button
- the fix-it button
- the responsibility button
- the incompetence button
- the guilt button
- the resentment button.

It's important for an assessor to know, as noted earlier in this discussion, that reflective functioning can be improved with practice, at least in most people. So the goal in an assessment setting is basically to assess a person's openness to the process of reflection and their willingness to work on strengthening their ability to think deeply about their relationships, both their parent–child relationship should they adopt and their adult partner relationships, which are so vital to parental teamwork. Perhaps in an interview a prospective adoptive or foster parent may say something like 'Well, I never thought about that, but I can see why it would be important for me to think more about my own experiences with my parents'. This is an indication, along with other signs of openness in the interview, that the person can see the value of self-reflection and is willing to work at strengthening their reflective capacity as part of the process of becoming an adoptive or foster parent.

## Conclusion

In short, the capacity to shift from self-protective, egocentric reactions to our children into a reflective state of mind in which we can reconnect with our deeper sense of purpose as a parent and with our deeper understanding of ourselves and our children is crucial to being able to parent well. Reflective functioning is especially crucial to parenting deeply mistrusting children. Stress can suppress the capacity to reflect, so it is important to assess prospective caregivers' ability to deal with stress effectively. Recent research indicates that reflective functioning can be improved with practice.

Reflective functioning is not a constant state of mind, but rather a state that needs to be 'reinstated' often, especially following disruptions or misattuned interactions in which the parent is likely, in the heat of the moment, to have experienced the child negatively and felt personally attacked or rejected. We cannot help feeling social pain, the pain of being rebuffed or 'put to the side' in the moment-to-moment interactions with our children, especially if we are parenting a child with blocked trust. The goal is to be compassionate with ourselves about having negative reactions to our child so that rather than immersing ourselves in the negative feelings or in guilt about having these feelings, we begin the shift from this egocentric, self-protective state into reflective mind, into that state of mind in which we recover our ability to understand our child's mistrust and to feel compassion based on knowing how his deep mistrust was forced upon him by poor care. This involves accessing knowledge that was temporarily out of mind, unavailable to us when we were in the throes of 'taking it personally'. By using reflective functioning regularly, parents can enhance their ability to parent in the caring, mindful way children need, especially children who are challenged to learn how to trust caregivers after early exposure to poor care.

## References

*Annals of the New York Academy of Sciences* (2014) 'Advances in meditation research.' volume 1307, Neuroscience and Clinical Applications.

Banfield, J., Wyland, C., Macrae, C., Munte, T. and Heatherton, T. (2004) 'The Cognitive Neuroscience of Self-regulation.' In R. Baumeister and K. Vohs (eds) *Handbook of Self-regulation.* New York: Guilford Press.

Chielsa, A. and Serretti, A. (2010) 'A systematic review of neurobiological and clinical features of mindfulness meditations.' *Psychological Medicine 40,* 1239–1252.

Davis, M. and Whalen, P. J. (2001) 'The amygdala: Vigilance and emotion.' *Molecular Psychiatry 6,* 13–34.

Fonagy, P., Gergely, G., Jurist, E. and Target, M. (2002) *Affect Regulation, Mentalization, and the Development of the Self.* New York: Other Press.

Frith, U. and Frith, C. D. (2003) 'Development and neurophysiology of mentalizing.' *Philosophical Transactions of the Royal Society of London. Series B: Biological Sciences 358,* 459–473.

Green, J., Leadbitter, K., Kay, C and Sharma, K. Autistic Spectrum Disorder in UK Adopted Children. Submitted to European Child and Adolescent Psychiatry.

Harris, B. (2003) *When Your Kids Push Your Buttons and What You Can Do About It.* New York: Warner Books.

Hughes, D. (2007) *Attachment-focused Family Therapy.* New York: Norton.

Hughes, D. (2009) *Attachment-focused Parenting.* New York: Norton.

Hughes, D. and Baylin, J. (2012) *Brain-based Parenting.* New York: Norton.

Lieberman, M.D. (2012) *Social: Why Our Brains Are Wired to Connect.* New York, NY: Random House.

Mascaro, J., Rilling, J., Negi, L. and Raison, C. (2013) 'Compassion meditation enhances empathic accuracy and related neural activity.' *Social Cognitive and Affective Neuroscience 8,* 48–55.

National Scientific Council on the Developing Child (2008) 'The timing and quality of early experiences combine to shape brain architecture.' Center on the Developing Child, Harvard University, Working Paper 5.

National Scientific Council on the Developing Child (2010) 'Early experiences can alter gene expression and affect long-term development.' Center on the Developing Child, Harvard University, Working Paper 10.

Siegel, D. (2014) *Brainstorm.* New York: Penguin Books.

Siegel, D. & Bryson, T.P. (2011) *The Whole-brain Child.* New York, NY: Delacorte.

Strathearn, L. and Fonagy, P. (2009) 'Adult attachment predicts maternal brain and oxytocin response to infant cues.' *Neuropsychopharmacology 34,* 2655–2666.

Tang, Y. Y., Rothbart, M. K. and Posner, M. J. (2012) 'Neural correlates of establishing, maintaining, and switching brain states.' *Trends in Cognitive Sciences 16,* 330–337.

Teicher, M. H., Andersen, S. L., Polcari, A., Anderson, C. M., Navalta, C. P. and Kim, D. M. (2003) 'The neurobiological consequences of early stress and childhood maltreatment.' *Neuroscience Biobehavioral Review 27,* 33–44.

Tronick, E. (2007) *The Neurobehavioral and Social-emotional Development of Infants and Children.* New York: Norton.

# CHAPTER 9

# Conclusion

*David Howe*

## Making sense

In all scientific endeavours, there is a restless interaction between theory, research and practice. In fields of enquiry that are relatively new, there tends to be a time lag between theory and research and any effective practices based on them. It takes a while for ideas and understandings to settle down and be accepted by most of those in the professional community.

Science proceeds when people are faced with a problem, tackle a puzzle, want an explanation or simply feel curious. Minds get to work and ponder what might be going on. And to help minds think better, people look and prod, explore and investigate, experiment and measure the things that puzzle and fascinate them. All of this activity generates a lot of description of the things under observation. In the early stages of most enquiries, one of the first things scientists do is try to find some basic order in all this observation and description. Types are identified. Classifications are made. Under each type or in each classification, things are put together that appear to have things in common. This then begs the question 'What might account for the similarities between things in the same category, and what might explain why things in a different category look, behave, interact differently?' One of my favourite examples of the value of organising things according to their properties and characteristics is Dmitri Mendeleev's periodic table of the natural elements. This extraordinary, beautiful classification of the elements marked the beginning of modern chemistry.

Although rarely pursued in neat, straight lines, most scientists and practitioners progress something along the following lines: they identify a problem, phenomenon or puzzle and wonder how it might be explained. The explanations suggest a theory or a hypothesis – I think this is what's going on here, or, I have a hunch this is why things might be behaving as they do. The behaviour, phenomenon or event is then observed, explored and subjected to experiment to see if the theory or hypothesis holds up under scrutiny. If it does, then this provides support for the theory. If it doesn't, then the theory either has to be modified, or may be ditched altogether.

Bringing the grand sweep of this kind of thinking nearer to home, developmental psychologists have applied similar methods to their work as they wonder how children grow and behave, how they learn and adapt, why they differ one from another and how life events impact on them, for good or ill. For example, it is recognised that children, as well as adults, vary in terms of their temperaments, and that in fact it is possible to categorise individuals in terms of where they lie along each one of five major temperamental or personality traits (openness to new experience–resistance to new experience; conscientiousness–impulsivity; extroversion–introversion; agreeableness–antagonism; and neuroticism–emotional stability). These traits seem to affect not only the children and their development but also the style and quality of the parenting they received.

## Attachment patterns and styles

In similar fashion, Mary Ainsworth, inspired by John Bowlby's early thinking about children and their attachment to parents, undertook some experimental observations, later confirmed in home observation studies, of children being separated from and then reunited with their parents (Ainsworth et al. 1978). Initially, she recognised three different kinds of behaviour and reactions to these separations and reunions. Some children showed appropriate distress upon separation but were soon comforted and regulated when the parent returned. These children she described as securely attached (the B pattern). Other children appeared to show little outward sign of upset when the parent departed. Nor did they look for comfort when the parent reappeared.

She classified these children as *avoidant* (the A pattern). Ainsworth also identified a third pattern. In this case, the children showed high levels of distress upon separation and even though they approached the parent for contact when reunited, they wouldn't be comforted or soothed. Their distress continued. Ainsworth classified these children as *ambivalent* (the C pattern). Avoidant and ambivalent children were both seen as insecurely attached.

Having offered this simple classification of different types of response and reaction to parental separations and reunions, the next question was 'What leads to, causes and lies behind these different attachment behaviours?' These early theories, research findings and classifications then spawned a huge amount of thinking and investigation. A few years later, a fourth category was added by Main and Solomon (1986). Children placed in this group reacted in a variety of odd ways when separated and seemed unable to find any behavioural strategy that would increase feelings of comfort when their parent returned. Children with these behaviours were described as having *disorganised* or *disoriented* attachments (the D pattern). This lack of an effective attachment strategy under stress was particularly common amongst children who had suffered traumatic loss, neglect or abuse. It was this group of children who seemed at greatest risk of poor mental health, behavioural problems and long-term psychopathology. And it was many of the children in this group who became increasingly likely to be considered for adoption and foster care as late-age placements.

So, bit by bit, it gradually became apparent that particular styles of parenting were associated with each attachment type (Solomon and George 1996; Howe 2011). Further thought and research found that open and sensitive, attuned and responsive parenting led to children feeling securely attached. These children can generally look forward to healthy psychosocial development.

Parents who are uncomfortable with their own as well as other people's emotions, who remain distant, even rejecting whenever their children make emotional overtures or behave in a vulnerable way, are likely to have children classified as avoidantly attached.

Parents who are liable to feel anxious, helpless and overwhelmed when faced with a needy, stressed, upset or vulnerable child tend to have babies who are classified as ambivalently attached.

These parents typically complain that they, too, feel emotionally neglected and undervalued and react to most stressful events with exaggerated upset and drama.

And as we have seen, disorganised children typically have parents who are abusive and dangerous (hostile and frightening) or neglectful and unavailable (helpless and frightened).

## Practical applications of developmental theories

These early research findings, classifications and explanations not only helped practitioners recognise and understand some of the differences found in children's development and behaviour, they also began to suggest what might be done in cases where help, support or treatment were called for. Attachment organisations can and do change over the lifecourse, particularly in the context of close relationships. These findings gave encouragement to practitioners. If good quality relationships can bring about changes in attachment organisation, then it behoves practitioners either to set about improving the quality of the caregiving skills of birth parents or, in more extreme cases, to remove children and place them with more skilled substitute parents and families.

Helping struggling parents of maltreated children to improve their caregiving skills is the preferred course of action, morally and developmentally. At its most simplistic, if sensitive and attuned parenting predicts securely attached children and if securely attached children can look forward to a mentally healthy life, then it seems sensible to help parents who lack sensitivity, attunement and empathy to acquire these skills so that their children can become more securely attached and more psychologically successful.

As the research continued, it also became apparent that many, if not most poorly skilled parents, especially those who either abused or neglected their children, themselves had suffered loss, rejection, abuse or neglect in their own childhoods. In short, their attachments were insecure, and most likely disorganised. Those who failed to resolve these early childhood losses and hurts were at greatest risk of poor mental health and insensitive, unattuned parenting.

However, adults who had experienced childhood maltreatment but who had been helped, usually in the context of a good, empathic relationship, to think about, reflect on and make sense of their early troubled lives were much more likely to develop a 'resolved' state of mind with respect to their childhood losses and hurts. These resolved states of mind – minds that could process difficult memories and feelings – were less defensive and more able to see, understand and empathise with other minds, including those of their own children. In other words, although these parents might have suffered loss and maltreatment as children, nevertheless they were now able to recognise and acknowledge the impact that these early experiences might continue to have on their present relationships, including those with their own children. This 'resolved' group of parents provided strong evidence that people in the context of a helpful, therapeutic relationship, could change.

The paradox, then, is the ability to recognise, reflect on and manage one's own vulnerabilities actually helps you improve your resilience, attunement and ability to be open. When parents' care becomes less 'blocked', they become more emotionally available for their children. As Kim S. Golding and Ben Gurney-Smith in Chapter 5 and Jonathan Baylin in Chapter 8 describe, parents who have these reflective skills (high reflective function), however acquired, tend to be more resilient and better able to stay with and tune into their children at times of stress. And in turn, their children are more likely to develop secure attachments with all their long-term benefits

These findings, therefore, suggest ways in which insecure, unresolved parents might be helped. If abused and neglected children could be helped by developing a relationship with a caring, interested, safe and mind-minded adult (an empathic teacher, a loving foster parent, a caring adopter, a talented psychotherapist, a concerned aunt), then the provision of such a mind-engaging relationship *at any point in the life course* might also be therapeutic. Ideally, therapists might try to work with birth parents to improve their sensitivity and mentalising skills, in which case children might be allowed to remain at home. But failing that, child care professionals working with maltreated children might need to think of removing the children and placing them with attuned foster carers or sensitive and open-minded adopters.

## Foster care and adoption for children with histories of abuse, neglect and trauma

But even as these ideas were evolving, it was also becoming apparent that the adaptive and defensive strategies that many abused, neglected and traumatised children developed in order to survive both physically and psychologically came with high developmental and relationship costs. You couldn't simply place these children with loving foster carers or adopters and expect them to drop their defences and ditch the strategies of survival they had developed in the context of abusive, rejecting and neglectful birth parenting (Howe 1998). These were children who had learned to survive by not trusting adults, never letting others get into positions of power and control, never showing need, never getting emotionally close, going it alone, and remaining ever alert to the presence of hurt and danger.

It soon became apparent that many, if not most children with histories of loss and maltreatment come to all new relationships with their defences raised. Developmentally traumatised children operate in survival mode however benign the context (see Chapter 2 by Kim S. Golding). They are wary, anxious, angry, needy, stressed, emotionally dysregulated and hurt. They find it difficult to calm down once they are aroused – and they are very easily aroused. Their only experience of being parented and emotionally close is that it feels potentially dangerous. Indeed, as Kim S. Golding and Ben Gurney-Smith remind us in Chapter 5, being parented for these children becomes a trigger for putting both the body and the mind into a state of alarm.

History, therefore, has taught these children that carers cannot and should not be trusted. So although new parents set out to be their child's greatest source of safety and comfort, the developmentally traumatised child, at least initially, will see them as the greatest source of potential hurt and danger. In short, developmentally traumatised children are frightened of being parented because all previous experiences of being parented have resulted in neglect, abuse, rejection and loss.

## The capacities and skills needed to parent children who have been abused, neglected and traumatised

Thus, as we have seen throughout the chapters of this book, even for secure, mind-minded new carers, these children are not easy to parent. Foster carers and adopters require all the skills that characterise the good enough carer. They need to tune into their child's views and perspective. They need to be able to mentalise and reflect on their own as well as the child's mind and behaviour. They need to be good 'people readers', to be empathic and to have 'mindsight'. However, it *is* a challenge to think about things from the child's point of view. It requires patience, and a willingness to acknowledge relationship errors. It involves repairing the damage that communication errors and breakdowns can cause.

In addition, as Julie Selwyn notes in Chapter 3, successful parents also need realistic expectations, flexible attitudes, high levels of tolerance, tenacity, the ability to manage stress, good support networks and a sense of humour. And even then, say Golding and Gurney-Smith in Chapter 5, there will be moments when parents feel helpless and at sea, guilty and hurt, stressed and tired. It is at such moments that their caring capacities become 'blocked' (see Chapters 5 and 6).

As Joanne Alper describes in Chapter 4, one of the key assessment tasks, therefore, is to explore how well prospective carers manage relationship stress in the present, as this predicts how well they are likely to manage the relationship stresses experienced with their children in the future.

The practice and presence of these therapeutic skills and behaviours is easier said than done, but parents who stick with them will find that their fostered or adopted child will gradually, ever so gradually, let their defences down. The child will slowly sense that the relationship with the new parent is safe, a place where they can begin to think about feelings and reflect on their own as well as other people's behaviour. In other words, once they can begin to allow the carer into their mind-space and body-space without feeling threatened, they will begin to develop some of the emotional and psychological skills that will help them self-regulate, empathise, reflect and show resilience. Not until you have been on the receiving end of relationships with skilled, mentalising, reflective and self-regulated others can you develop these skills yourself. And once you have acquired these skills, your mental health will begin to improve, your developmental prospects will look up, and your relationships will get better. But all of this takes time, and behaviourally speaking, for every two steps taken forward, developmentally traumatised children typically take at least one step back.

That's the ideal prospect for children placed with reasonably regulated, emotionally intelligent foster carers and adopters. However, even in these cases, parents will need to draw on all their strengths as well as the support of family, friends and community, and the advice and help of foster care and adoption specialists.

It is when hurt and traumatised children are placed with new carers who are less robust, less able to mentalise and reflect openly on their own and their child's thoughts and feelings, that there is the danger that the stresses experienced by both parent and child will trigger more defensive behaviours and less effective ways of relating by both parties. Under stress, insecure and unresolved parents are less able to think, assess and empathise. They begin to feel either helpless or hostile, or both.

These parental responses, of course, are familiar territory for the child who has suffered abuse and neglect. When carers react with anger and distress, unable to regulate their own feelings never mind those of their child, then the placed child will simply activate all their old, well-established survival strategies and behaviours – coercion, control, aggression, sarcasm, denial, avoidance, withdrawal, dissociation, insatiable demands. At this point, when both parent and child find themselves in escalating states of emotional dysregulation, connections are lost, the capacity to reflect is no longer present, and learning ceases. The child feels unmanageable and out of control. And there is the real danger that the placement will break down.

## Assessments, analysis and education of prospective foster carers and adopters

All of which brings us to the point of this book. If children with histories of trauma, loss and hurt are to enjoy successful placements, they need to join families in which parents have good mentalising skills that allow them to reflect, connect, understand, process, engage, regulate and repair without too much defensiveness or distortion (see Chapter 4 by Joanne Alper).

These are parents who know to have fun and be *Playful*, who *Accept* their child's inner world, who are *Curious* about their child's behaviour and who possess *Empathy* (for fuller accounts of PACE, see Hughes 2009; Golding and Hughes 2012, and Chapters 4, 5 and 6 of this book).

The ideal, of course, is to identify and select secure parents with these capacities at the assessment stage. There are wonderfully gifted people out there, but many people, perhaps the majority, don't quite tick all of the boxes that define the authoritative, unblocked, resilient, attuned and reflective parent. But they are, in Winnicott's immortal phrase, 'good enough'.

Would-be carers who are assessed as basically secure, emotionally skilled and 'good enough' will be open to new learning. They will be quick to understand how their prospective child's past losses and hurts will have left them needy and vulnerable, angry and wary, frightened and defensive. They will recognise that under stress their child's behaviour will become challenging and their emotions unmanageable.

These 'good enough' prospective carers will also understand that there will be times when their child's needs and behaviours will overwhelm and dysregulate them as parents. But because they have the psychological skills and resources that allow them to think about, process and reflect on their own reactions as well their child's needs and behaviour, their natural resilience will reassert itself. They will recover, repair the damage of any broken communication and reconnect, seek support, and once more become that safe haven and secure base that their child so desperately craves, but can't always trust (Schofield and Beek 2014). They offer, as Kim S. Golding puts it in Chapter 2, therapeutic or healing parenting, parenting that takes into account the impact of early life trauma on their children's development, needs and behaviour.

As we noted above, at the other extreme, there will be a few prospective carers in the assessment process who will have suffered major loss, rejection or hurt in their own childhoods. A few will have resolved these painful memories and will therefore be assessed as secure. These 'resolved' applicants will, in all likelihood, become effective parents.

But for others, the impact of their early troubled care-receiving experiences continues to remain unrecognised, unacknowledged, unresolved or unprocessed. Under relationship stress, these adults lose the capacity to mentalise. They can no longer reflect on and process what is happening to them and the other. Many placed children, perhaps the majority, will very easily and quickly trigger these unresolved, anxious or dismissing states of mind in their carers. In effect, these are people who, under relationship stress, find that their ability to mentalise goes 'off-line' (Fonagy 2006). Caught up in the stress of the relationship, the parent feels helpless and hostile. The placed child once again finds themselves alone, frightened, angry and unable to reflect or self-regulate. If the practitioner's assessment and analysis suggests that the applicant has an unresolved state of mind with respect to past painful memories and whose care is likely to become 'blocked' under stress, then that applicant should be helped to withdraw.

However, in the middle will be found many people who lie somewhere in the attachment range of secure to mildly insecure, people who might not always react with the greatest skill under emotional stress – but they know it, acknowledge it and are willing to do something about it. The assessment therefore recognises that they are willing and able to learn – about themselves and about the kind of children who are likely to be placed with them. It is their basic emotional intelligence and capacity to mentalise that allows them to be open about their own and other people's thoughts and feelings, behaviours and understandings, strengths and weaknesses. They can learn. They want to learn – about themselves, about how their own relationship past impacts on their present thoughts and feelings, about how children can affect their parenting strengths and weaknesses. They feel they can change. These self-same skills and capacities are those that will stand them in good stead when parenting the placed child. And it is these kinds of parenting skills and talents that placed children need if they are to develop and resolve their own troubled memories.

As Julie Selwyn and Joanne Alper observe, simple descriptions of the applicants' history, characteristics and circumstances are not enough (see Chapters 3 and 4). The key assessment task is to *analyse* the mass of descriptive content generated during the assessment process, including assessing the prospective carer's attachment history and current attachment style (see Chapter 6 by Dan Hughes).

Thus, the aims of the assessor and her analysis are (1) to identify those applicants who either have, or demonstrate the potential to have these reflective and mentalising capacities; (2) to help applicants recognise and understand their own psychological strengths and weaknesses; (3) to help applicants recognise, understand and make sense of the suboptimal developmental pathways followed by most placed children and how this affects their thinking, feelings and relationship behaviour, (4) to help applicants anticipate and explore how placed children with these troubled histories will affect them as people, parents and partners; and (5) to help applicants develop the kind of skills, understandings and capacities that will not only help them to live with their children, but will also promote their children's own emotional and relationship skills so that they, too, will grow up to be secure and mentally healthy adults.

## The coming together of the developmental sciences to support an integrated approach to more analytic assessments

As we hinted at the beginning of this chapter, supporting the idea of the kind of assessments and analyses outlined in this book is a growing body of theory and research across a range of developmental disciplines. The importance of the early parent–child relationship continues to be recognised by both developmental scientists and mental health practitioners.

Developmental psychologists understand that children don't develop relationships skills, emotional competence and mentalising capacities unless they have been on the receiving end of such experiences. Parents who have these capacities also help their children learn to self-regulate physically, emotionally and cognitively. Children who learn to self-regulate experience less stress, cope better with new experiences, and enjoy their bodies and minds operating as one. The analytic assessment process is premised on these insights and understandings.

As Jonathan Baylin explores in his two chapters (Chapters 7 and 8), brain scientists now recognise that early experiences also affect children's neurological development. Children who suffer regular and frequent high levels of stress in relationships with primary caregivers who are rejecting, abusive and neglectful risk a range of compromises to their brain's ability to function effectively. Much of the young child's brain is programmed to make sense of experience, but before it can make sense of that experience, it needs exposure to the experience of which it needs to make sense. This is true of many physical, sensory and psychological experiences including the ability to recognise, process and regulate emotions. Children who have enjoyed empathic, reflective, emotionally skilled parenting themselves tend to become empathic, reflective and emotionally skilled.

A basic understanding of how the brain grows, develops and functions under different caregiving and relationship regimes can therefore usefully inform the analytic assessor's thinking (see Chapter 7 by Jonathan Baylin; see also Hughes and Baylin 2012). Indeed, in Chapter 7, Jonathan Baylin invites assessors to think of the assessment process itself as a 'stress test' for gathering information about the health of the applicant's brain! Prospective carers also find these ideas both fascinating and helpful.

And finally, there is growing evidence that the quality of gene expression is also affected by the quality of the environment in which genes find themselves. How genes get switched on and off is affected by such things as diet, pollution and smoking. But many genes, including many of those that are involved in stress regulation and the healthy functioning of the immune system, are also affected by the child's emotional and relationship environment. Stressful environments of neglect and abuse can negatively affect how certain genes get either switched on or off during the course of a child's development. The long-terms effects of this not only compromise the child's mental health but also their physical and medical health prospects throughout the lifecourse. Although this research does not directly affect the assessment of prospective foster carers and adopters, it adds yet another plank supporting the idea that all children need good quality, attuned, well-regulated relationships if they are to grow up in the best of health, and that it is never too late to benefit from this kind of parenting even if you have suffered loss, abuse and neglect in your early years.

The previous chapters capture the thinking and wisdom of pioneering practices that are being inspired by some of the cutting edge thinking and research being generated by developmental psychologists and developmental neuroscientists. Over the last 40 or 50 years we have recognised some of the key ingredients that make for effective parenting. We have also learned how deep can be the developmental damage experienced by children who have suffered abuse, neglect and trauma.

More recent research is showing us how these developmentally traumatised and troubled children can be helped when they are placed with empathic, mindsightful, responsive new carers. But this same research is also telling us that even carers whose reflective functions are high will experience moments of stress and feelings of helplessness and anger as they care for their fostered and adopted children. It is at these moments that carers have to recover their capacities to reflect, think, connect, repair and seek support. Recovery of these capacities not only restores empathy, openness and understanding, it also helps the child return to a place of emotional safety. When the parent is once more a safe haven, children can use them as a secure base from which to explore their own and other people's thoughts, feelings and behaviour. The safe haven is that place in which troubled children can be helped to regulate their minds and bodies. It is where they can practise their reflective thinking.

The analytic assessment process therefore seeks to identify prospective carers who have, or who have the potential to develop these developmentally beneficial parenting skills (see Chapter 4). The assessment also weaves into its practices a strong educational element in which applicants have the opportunity to learn about and understand the developmentally traumatised child, their own psychological make-up, their relationship style, and their own strengths and weaknesses, especially under conditions of stress.

If we are to help the developmentally traumatised child heal and get back onto a developmentally optimal track, it is vital that the assessments of prospective carers are not only rich in description and sound on classification but also analytically smart, for the sake of the child, the carers and society.

# References

Ainsworth, M., Blehar, M., Waters, E. and Wall, S. (1978) *Patterns of Attachment: A Psychological Study of the Strange Situation.* Hillsdale, NJ: Erlbaum.

Fonagy, P. (2006) 'The Mentalization-focused Approach to Social Development.' In J. Allen and P. Fonagy (eds) *Handbook of Mentalization-based Treatment.* Chichester: John Wiley.

Golding, K. and Hughes, D. (2012) *Creating Loving Attachments: Parenting with PACE to Nurture Confidence and Security in the Troubled Child.* London: Jessica Kingsley Publishers.

Howe, D. (1998) *Patterns of Adoption: Nature, Nurture and Psychosocial Development.* Chichester: Wiley.

Howe, D. (2011) *Attachment Across the Lifecourse: A Brief Introduction.* Basingstoke: Palgrave Macmillan.

Hughes. D. (2009) *Attachment Focused Parenting: Effective Strategies to Care for Children.* New York: W.W. Norton.

Hughes, D. and Baylin, J. (2012) *Brain-based Parenting.* New York: Norton.

Main, M. and Solomon, J. (1986) 'Discovery of an Insecure-Disorganized/Disoriented Pattern.' In T. Brazleton and M. Yogman (eds) *Affective Development in Infancy.* Norwood, NJ: Ablex.

Schofield, G. and Beek, M. (2014) *The Secure Base Model: Promoting Attachment and Resilience in Foster Care and Adoption.* London: BAAF.

Solomon, J. and George, C. (1996) 'Defining the caregiving system: Toward a theory of caregiving.' *Infant Mental Health Journal 17,* 183–197.

# CONTRIBUTORS

**Joanne Alper** is Director of Services at Adoptionplus. She had a central role in the establishment of Adoptionplus as a voluntary adoption agency offering a new type of adoption placement service in the UK, one that provides access to ongoing therapeutic support to adoptive families throughout childhood. Joanne is responsible for developing the Placement Service, Children and Family Therapy Service, the Birth Relative Counselling Service and the Training Service at Adoptionplus. She has had a number of books published in this field – six books in the *Billy Says* series and *All about Mummies and Daddies*. Joanne is a qualified social worker and play therapist whose previous career covered managing a fostering team within the independent sector, managing a looked-after children team within a local authority, working in child protection for five years and practising as an independent play therapist.

**Dr Jonathan Baylin** received his doctorate in clinical psychology from Peabody College of Vanderbilt University in 1981. He has been working in the mental health field for 35 years. For the past 15 years, while continuing his clinical practice, he has immersed himself in the study of neurobiology and in teaching mental health practitioners about the brain. He has given numerous workshops for mental health professionals on 'putting the brain in therapy'. Several years ago, Dr Baylin began a collaborative relationship with Dan Hughes, a leader in the field of attachment-focused therapy. Their book, *Brain-based Parenting*, was released by Norton Press in the spring of 2012 as part of the Norton series on Interpersonal Neurobiology edited by Daniel Siegel, MD. Dr Baylin has delivered the keynote sessions at the Association for Treatment and Training in the Attachment of Children (ATTACh) and North American Council on Adoptable Children (NACAC) annual conferences, presenting his model of the neurobiology of caregiving, attachment and attachment-focused treatment. He has also given numerous workshops both internationally and regionally within the United States. He has developed a brain-based model of attachment-focused treatment to help therapists and caregivers facilitate the child's journey from mistrust to trust.

**Dr Kim S. Golding** is a clinical psychologist who lives in Worcestershire, England. Kim has always been interested in parenting, and collaborating with parents or carers to develop their parenting skills tailored to the particular needs of the children they are caring for. She is trained and certified in dyadic developmental practice (DDP) and is involved in certifying and training other professionals in this approach. Kim, alongside a small group of colleagues, is actively developing DDP within the UK. Kim has written a range of books on attachment, adoption and fostering including *Nurturing Attachments* and, with Dan Hughes, *Creating Loving Attachments*. She has developed a group work programme for foster carers and adopters, 'The Nurturing Attachments Training Resource'.

**Dr David Howe** is Emeritus Professor in the School of Social Work at the University of East Anglia, Norwich. He has research and writing interests in social work, emotional development, empathy, attachment theory, and child abuse and neglect. His most recent books include *Child Abuse and Neglect: Attachment, Development and Intervention* (2005), *The Emotionally Intelligent Social Worker* (2008), *A Brief Introduction to Social Work Theory* (2009), *Attachment Across the Lifecourse: A Brief Introduction* (2011), *Empathy: What It Is and Why It Matters* (2012) and *The Compleat Social Worker* (2014).

**Dan Hughes**, PhD, is a clinical psychologist with a limited practice near Philadelphia. He founded and developed DDP, the treatment of children who have experienced abuse and neglect and demonstrate ongoing problems related to attachment and trauma. This treatment occurs in a family setting and the treatment model has expanded to become a general model of family treatment. He has conducted seminars and workshops, and spoken at conferences throughout the United States, Europe, Canada and Australia for the past 17 years. He is also engaged in extensive training with certification of therapists in his treatment model, along with ongoing consultation for various agencies and professionals. Dan is the author of many books and articles. These include *Building the Bonds of Attachment* (2nd edition) (2006), *Attachment-Focused Parenting* (2009), *Attachment-Focused Family Therapy Workbook* (2011) and, with Jonathan Baylin, *Brain-based Parenting* (2012). Dan can be contacted at: dhughes202@comcast.net. His website is www.danielhughes.org.

**Professor Julie Selwyn** is Director of the Hadley Centre for Adoption and Foster Care Studies in the School for Policy Studies at the University of Bristol. Before joining the University, Julie worked as a children's social worker and residential worker for 15 years. She has published widely on substitute care including: the placement of minority ethnic children; studies of young people's view of foster care; outcomes for older children placed for adoption; contact; and the recruitment of minority ethnic adopters. She led a BIG lottery-funded study on kinship care, which for the first time used census data to calculate the number of kinship carers. Research findings can be accessed at www.bristol.ac.uk/hadley. Julie is a member of the national Adoption Leadership Board, and has recently completed a study of adoption disruption in England.

**Dr Ben Gurney-Smith** is a consultant clinical psychologist who leads the Therapy Service at Adoptionplus and has many years of supervised practice in DDP. Prior to his current role, Ben managed a dedicated service for looked-after and adopted children in Oxford, and acted as an expert witness in child care proceedings. This experience has given him a deep appreciation of children who enter care and the services they and their adoptive families deserve and require. Alongside clinical practice, Ben has a long-standing research interest in what makes adoptive parenting unique and, supported by these findings, he has overseen interventions that are informed by an understanding of attachment at the psychological and neurobiological levels. In this way, he has led innovation in the evaluation of 'The Nurturing Attachments Training Resource' by Kim S. Golding and interventions that address parenting stress directly such as mindfulness. He is a visiting tutor at the Oxford Doctoral Course in Clinical Psychology and contributes regularly to training in the clinical application of attachment theory.

# INDEX